KNOWING GOD'S LOVE

BY STEVE DEMME

This book is dedicated to my ever supportive, always faithful, loving wife and my patient, forgiving, teachable sons who learned along with me.

May it encourage those families whose hearts have been turned towards God and towards each other.

"Let the words of my mouth and the meditation of my heart be acceptable in your sight, O LORD, my rock and my redeemer." (Psalms 19:14)

KNOWING GOD'S LOVE

INTRODUCTION TO KNOWING GOD'S LOVE

This book is my journey of how God led me to understand the love of the Father and the grace of Jesus in a deeper way.

I firmly believe that comprehending God's unconditional love is the cornerstone for the overarching commands to love God and our neighbor. For we are unable to love until we have first been loved. "We love, because He first loved us." (1 John 4:19) and "In this is love, not that we have loved God but that he loved us." (1 John 4:10)

Beginning in 2009 I rediscovered the most important commandment. The first, or as Jesus called it, the Great Command, is to love God with everything in me. As I thought about the importance of loving God, I realized I had rarely stopped to reflect if I did love Him. I was aware of believers in the church at Ephesus who had lost their first love (Revelation 2:4) and not wanting to be like them, began asking God to help me love Him with all my heart, soul, mind, and strength.

I was wonderfully surprised by how he answered my request. Instead of awaking one morning with a burning love for God, which is how I expected Him to answer, He began to steadily reveal how much He loved me. In 2012 I found myself believing God genuinely loves me. This knowledge that God likes me for who I am, and not based on what I do, has transformed my life.

My relationship with God is now much richer and deeper. My wife and I are closer than we have ever been and are enjoying a rebirth in our marriage. I am able to communicate and connect with my sons with honesty and openness. Knowing I am loved and accepted just as I am, has freed me to be more transparent and real as I relate with others.

In the past, when I was asked to summarize my vision for the family I would respond, "Where each lives for the other, and all live for Christ." With my eyes opened to the First and Great Command, loving God with everything in us, and the New Command, loving each other as God has loved us, I have revised my vision. I now believe a biblical vision for building a family of faith is: where each loves God with all their heart, soul, mind, and strength, and all love each other as God has loved them. I also believe the only way to fulfill these two commands and build a Godly family is to first be loved by God. We can only give what we have received.

If I only had time to deliver one message, before I passed on to the next life, it would be that God likes His children. Whether I am addressing audiences or conversing with individuals, I have a strong desire to share this simple but profound truth: God not only loves us, He genuinely likes us.

Since this book was first published, I have added a one hour talk on the same subject online. You may watch it here http://www.buildingfaithfamilies.org/

knowinggodslove/. Other material will continue to be added here in the future.

Prayer

As you read this book, it is my hope "that according to the riches of his glory, He may grant you to be strengthened with power through His Spirit in your inner being, that you, being rooted and grounded in love, may have strength to comprehend with all the saints what is the breadth and length and height and depth, and to know the love of Christ that surpasses knowledge, that you may be filled with all the fullness of God." (Ephesians 3:16–19)

CHAPTER OVERVIEW

There are two preeminent, all encompassing commands for every believer: Love God with everything in us, and love others as we have been loved by God. Jesus refers to them as the First or Great Command, and the New Command. I have learned I am unable to love God or others until I have first been loved by Him. "We love, because He first loved us." (1 John 4:19) The degree to which I am loved by God determines my capacity to love God and others.

When I began to have my eyes opened to the importance of loving God, I realized I had not given much intentional thought to this fundamental command. I knew when Jesus was asked what the great command was, he quoted Deuteronomy 6:5. "He said to him, 'You shall love the Lord your God with all your heart and with all your soul and with all your mind.'" Then, in Matthew 22:38 "This is the great and first commandment."

I don't ever recall asking myself if I did love Him, or to what degree, or how to demonstrate this love. I did give more thought about what Jesus referred to as the second command, "A second is like it: You shall love your neighbor as yourself." (Matthew 22:39)

Because of Mathew 22:40, "On these two commandments depend all the Law and the Prophets," I preached a sermon on how each of the ten commandments could be classified as an extension of loving God or loving our neighbor. For example, if you love God, you won't take His name in vain or worship idols. If you love your neighbor, you won't murder him, or covet his belongings.

This book is my journey of learning to love God with all my heart, soul, mind, and strength, and how to love my wife and children as God has loved me. Following, is a brief summary of each chapter to give you an overview of what you will be reading.

In **Chapter 1, Meeting Jesus**, God orchestrated several events to open my eyes to the need for improving my relationship with my heavenly Father. As I sought God for help in loving Him, He answered my requests, just not as I expected.

In **Chapter 2, Surprised by God's Good News**, the scales continued to fall off my eyes as the good Spirit expanded my understanding of the gospel. I received new insights into the grace of God and the depth of the good news in not only taking away my sin, but in making me pleasing in His sight.

The verse which has meant the most to me on this journey, and which we will explore in **Chapter 3, As the Father Loved Me**, is John 15:9, "As the Father has loved me, so have I loved you. Abide in my love." I must have read that chapter at least thirty-five times over the past third of a century, but I had missed this verse. As much as God the Father loves Jesus the Son, Jesus the Son loves you and me. Amazing.

In **Chapter 4, The Identity of the Son of God**, we discuss the baptism of Jesus. There, His Father in heaven spoke, "This is my beloved Son." When we are adopted into the family of God through the sacrificial death of Jesus, His Spirit witnesses to our spirit, that we are children of God. Knowing that we are not only followers and disciples of Jesus, but adopted children, significantly changes our perception of God as our Father.

"You do not have, because you do not ask." (James 4:2) A similar thought is expressed in John 16:24, "Ask, and you will receive, that your joy may be full." In 2009, I began asking the living God to help me comprehend His love. I regularly thought about Ephesians 3:14–19 as well as verses like these two from James and John. As I asked, God illuminated biblical truths to me in such a way that the eternal verities of the word and the character of God came to life in a new way. **Chapter 5, Illuminations and Knowing God**, has several of these experiences described, in hopes that they will bless you as they have blessed me.

Throughout 2012, God gave me several tastes of His love. But the call of John 15:9 is to not merely taste and see that God is good, but to "abide in His love." I discuss abiding in **Chapter 6, Abide, Dwell, Live and Remain in My Love**. To abide is the call of God to not simply have special forays into experiencing His affection, but daily living and abiding at a different plane. I have found this takes work, the work of abiding.

From daily meditations, to reflection, to scripture studies, to quietly waiting on God, I will try to explain what I have discovered on my journey about dwelling and remaining in God's love, in hopes that you will be encouraged in your walk with God.

Chapter 7, Know the Truth to Be Set Free, addresses transformation and truth. Jesus told a group of religious people that the truth would set them free. They protested that they already were children of Abraham and did not need any help. I too thought I knew a good bit, but as I immersed myself in scripture, the truth indeed transformed my thinking and set me free from unscriptural beliefs that I was still embracing.

Believing that God loves me takes effort and intentionality. I have much less trouble believing that God loves my wife and children. I have little difficulty believing that He loves my brothers and sisters around the world. The battle of faith, is having assurance that He loves me. Thanks be to God for giving us His inspired word, for "faith comes from hearing, and hearing through the word of Christ." (Romans 10:17) In **Chapter 8, Faith Comes By Hearing the Word of Christ**, we will examine several passages that will strengthen our faith.

This is a portion of Paul's inspired prayer, "may have strength to comprehend with all the saints what is the breadth and length and height and depth, and to know the love of Christ." (in Ephesians 3:18–19) Each blood bought believer is a part of the body of Christ. We each supply something of value to the other members. We need each other's help grasping and comprehending the incredible dimensions of the love of Christ. I have been helped by wonderfully gifted people the world labels disabled. I am happy to share what they have taught me about unconditional love in **Chapter 9, Comprehending With All the Saints**.

One Sunday, as the main service was coming to a close, the pastor had us bow our heads for the benediction. I often miss these words as I am distracted thinking about who I am going to speak to after the service or what I am going to do after I get home. But that day, his words came to me in a powerful way. The pronouncement was taken from the last verse in 2 Corinthians. "The grace of the Lord Jesus Christ and the love of God and the fellowship of the Holy Spirit be with you all." (2 Corinthians 13:14) I had been comprehending the love of God, but I also recognized I had been receiving new insights into the grace of Jesus. In **Chapter 10, The Grace of Jesus**, I will share more insights into the unconditional love and grace of the Son.

The last phrase of 2 Corinthians 13:14 also was brought to life "the fellowship of the Holy Spirit be with you all." Other versions read, "the communion of the Holy Spirit." Because of this inspired phrase and other mentions of the Spirit in conjunction with understanding eternal truths, I have entered into a new understanding and relationship with the Spirit. Upon further study, I believe Jesus was helping to fulfill His destiny with the fellowship of the Spirit, and I know I need His presence and power to be who God designed me to be. I am happy to share what I am learning about my new friend, the Comforter and Helper, in **Chapter 11, Spirit of God**.

Many times I have attended a service where the preacher will knock on the podium and say something like God is knocking on the door of your heart, but it is up to each of us to open the door and invite Him to come in. The verse which is quoted is found in the letter to the Laodiceans in Revelation 3:20. The assumption is that God is calling non-believers to receive Jesus as their savior.

In truth, the passage is written "to the angel of the church in Laodicea." It is possible for believers to let Jesus remain outside the door and not allow Him to come in and share a meal with us. We have the ability to keep Jesus at arm's length. I have found God desires a close walk with me, but it is up to me to let God love me to open the door. Read more about this idea in **Chapter 12, Let God Love You**.

We all recognize we live in a culture which has warped and twisted the way people look at love. This is perhaps an over-generalization, but parents are told to give their children every desire to show their affection. Yet in the divine economy, God reveals his love by disciplining us. This process, while not enjoyable, is nonetheless extremely loving and for our good in the long run. May God give us eyes to discern the heart of God while enduring the hard experiences of correction and discipline. In **Chapter 13, God Is Treating You as Sons**, we remember, God is love, and He never changes.

Chapter 14, Possibly the Most Important Chapter, delves deeper into the power of the gospel. As much as non believers need to hear the good news of salvation through Jesus the Christ, so too do those who are already believers. In this section I will be relating incidents and obstacles to receiving grace and my need for more good news! Perhaps there are obstacles keeping me from accepting the truth of His unconditional love. Maybe I am too hard on myself and unable to receive forgiveness. I have asked God to search me and know my heart and reveal areas of need which keep me from comprehending the truth.

In Chapter 15, Why is Knowing God's Love Important? I will explore more about what it means to be rooted and grounded in the love of God. I also discuss many positive fruits I have experienced as a result of abiding in His love and burrowing deeper into grace.

Chapter 16, The Love of God Leads to the Knowledge of God is about the wonderfully surprising yet unlooked for fruit of being loved by God. The more I comprehend the divine affection of my Dad, my Brother, and my Friend the more I am learning about their character and personality.

CHAPTER 1:
MEETING JESUS

When I was 14 years old, I was invited by my friend Kevin, who was my mischievous partner-in-crime from Sunday school, to spend a week at a ranch in Colorado. I didn't know anything about the camp except the opportunity to attend was a really good deal. Kevin's aunt and uncle had offered to pay for him to attend the camp so he could hear the gospel. They also generously offered to pay for him to bring along a friend. I was the friend.

So in the summer of 1968, I boarded a Greyhound bus in Pittsburgh, Pennsylvania and began a three day journey to Colorado. I'd never been west of the Mississippi River. I also didn't know anyone on the bus except Kevin. As I began to meet the other kids on the bus, I noticed a different spirit about them. I also found out we were headed to a Christian camp.

Interestingly, no one asked me if I were a "Christian" or a "believer." After years of attending Sunday school, I would have answered in the affirmative. At some point I was asked if I had met Jesus. This question went to my heart, because I couldn't say I had. I knew about Jesus, but I had never had a personal encounter with Him nor could I say I knew Him.

A significant factor in this life changing week was the setting for the camp. The ranch was nestled in the Rocky Mountains, a few hours drive south of

Denver. I never tired of gazing at the panorama of the mountains and surrounding area. The landscape had a profound effect on me and made me aware of God in a way I had never experienced. When I laid eyes on the Rocky Mountains, it expanded something inside of me. They are so majestic and awesome and they made me aware of how big God is. "The invisible things of Him since the creation of the world are clearly seen, being perceived through the things that are made, even His everlasting power and divinity." (Romans 1:20)

During the meetings which we all attended and in our small get togethers in our cabin, I began learning about the different components of the Good News. I learned I could have my sins forgiven. This was very appealing since I knew I was not a good kid. I had been suspended from school at age 12, and it seemed like I was always apologizing to someone for breaking something or throwing something at some neighbor's kid. At camp I heard I could have a new beginning. Later, I was taught more about sin and disobedience to God's law, but at this juncture, I simply wanted a clean slate and a fresh start.

I also heard I would be able to know Jesus personally and talk to him as if He were sitting next to me. Even though I had many acquaintances, I didn't have a really close friend or a bosom buddy. I was a kind of loner, even though I didn't like being really alone. When I heard this part of the Good News, I knew I wanted a friend like Jesus. It says in the Bible He would never leave me or forsake me, so I would never be alone again.

I also believed if I invited Him into my heart I would have eternal life and go to heaven. This was not very applicable to me at such a young age, but it sounded good. However, what was even more appealing to me was that by having Jesus take my sins away and be with me always, I would have a joy and a peace which was different and deeper than anything the world had to offer.

When I put all the pieces together I thought, "Wow! Which part of this message isn't good?" Now I know why "the gospel" means "the good news." Yet, there was still a conflict in my soul. After some internal wrestling, I knew I wanted to respond to the gift Jesus was offering. The speakers at camp said Jesus was standing at the door of my heart gently knocking and desiring to come in, but it was up to me to open the door and invite Him in.

After a few days I made my way to a secluded part of the camp, behind a little Swiss chalet, on the side of a mountain. I asked Jesus to forgive my sins and come into my heart. He did and I knew it. I don't think I can explain how I knew, but I knew that He was real and He had indeed come into my innermost being. This when I invited Jesus to take up residence in my heart.

While I was at the camp, I learned a song, entitled "He's Everything To Me," by Ralph Carmichael. It was newly penned and not yet in any of the songbooks. Someone made copies on white mimeographed paper with purple letters. Older folks will recall this kind of copy which smelled so good when it was wet, just coming off the machine.

In the stars His handiwork I see,
  On the wind He speaks with majesty.

Though He ruleth over land and sea,
  What is that to me?

I will celebrate Nativity,
  For it has a place in history,

Sure, He came to set His people free,
  What is that to me?

Till by faith I met Him face to face,
  And I felt the wonder of His grace,

Then I knew that He was more than
  just a God who didn't care,

  Who lived a way up there, and

Now He walks beside me day by day,
  Ever watching o'er me lest I stray,

Helping me to find that narrow way,
  He's everything to me.

That song captured my encounter with Jesus. I knew there was a God "way up there," and I knew about Easter and Christmas. But then in 1968, on a mountain in Colorado, I met Him face to face and experienced the wonder of His grace and my life has never been the same.

That fall I entered high school and after three years moved on to college. During those years I had some special times of sensing God's presence at Christian retreats and Young Life gatherings in people's homes, but I was not a committed follower of Jesus. I remember, during one meeting, the speaker talked about all the things we run after to find fulfillment. Some try to acquire money as a way to be happy. Others think if they can find the perfect spouse they will be content. And the list goes on: recognition, sports, cars, etc.

During my junior year at Grove City College, just north of Pittsburgh, I felt like I had all the world had to offer. I was very involved in the life of the school, I served as president of the fraternity, vice-president of student government, and held other offices. I had a beautiful girlfriend, ran my own business in the summers, and had my own car. Life looked rosy on the outside. God was not very real to me, but it was because I had kept Him at arm's length. Yet in my innermost being I knew all this world had to offer did not satisfy my deepest longings. Behind the Swiss chalet in Colorado I had tasted the reality of God. I had met Jesus. As good as my life looked on the surface, I was not satisfied and knew there was something, or someone more.

After my junior year I applied to be a counselor at a camp in the Pocono Mountains working with troubled teens. In preparation for this job I read The Cross and the Switchblade by David Wilkerson. Part of the way through the book, I stopped reading and prayed, "Okay God, here we go." It was not a long prayer, but God knew what I meant. I wanted to follow Jesus fully and seek first His Kingdom, not my own kingdom or the kingdom of this world. I believe this was the time when Jesus became not just my part time savior and friend, but my full time Lord and master.

My last year at Grove City College was a wonderful time of personal growth. I had four close Christian bothers, Dan, Joe, Rick, and Andy, and we met regularly for Bible study and even organized a retreat for the men in our fraternity. Dr. Charles MacKenzie, the president of the university, and Dr. Bruce Thielemann, our chaplain, became lifelong friends and mentors. I was growing in my understanding of what it meant to serve God. My favorite verse became, "Seek first the kingdom." (Matthew 6:33) I was committed to serving God fully, and so when I graduated I made plans to attend Gordon-Conwell Theological Seminary, in South Hamilton, Massachusetts, to prepare for whatever field of service God opened up for me.

Those few years of seminary flew by, and with my new bride Sandi, entered the pastoral ministry.

We laid our life down to serve God by helping others. While living in a parsonage, God gave us four wonderful sons. We engaged in pastoral ministry, led summer camps for children and teens, opened our home to single adults and elderly saints, participated in summer Bible training for adults, served on the board of a children's home in India, and participated in the political process at our capitol, among other activities.

While I was seeking first the kingdom, over the years, a little distance had entered into my relationship with my Lord. I didn't stop to articulate what I was feeling, but rarely felt as if I were doing enough. No matter what I did, I felt driven to do more. Perhaps God was a little disappointed with me as I had not lived up to His expectations. I thought I would never quite measure up and kept trying to do more to please Him.

God was certainly not as real or as intimate to me as He was when I first heard the good news in Colorado. When I heard the gospel many years prior, I had no question at all Jesus loved me and wanted to have a relationship with me. I knew He was the loving father of the prodigal son standing there with arms wide open to receive me as I asked Him into my heart.

My Relationship with God

I know I was saved by grace alone, but at some point I began believing God loved me more when I did more wonderful things for Him. Even though I knew in my head God's love for me was based on grace, which is unconditional, somehow, I thought He would love me more if I behaved better or I did more for Him. Without recognizing this error, my relationship had subtly changed from unconditional love and acceptance, to God loving me and being pleased with me based on how I acted. Instead of a relationship rooted in what Jesus did, it now depended in part on what Steve did.

I had been learning that God loved me in my head, but I wasn't sensing this same love in my heart. An old proverb says, "The greatest journey a man will ever make is the eighteen inches from his head to his heart." I was aware of scriptures which convinced me theologically of God's care for me, but there is a big difference between head knowledge and heart understanding. So I began to seek God and ask Him to help me comprehend His love in a new way so I would believe in my heart, what I knew in my head.

John Teaches Me About Unconditional Love

Our fourth son, John, has Down's Syndrome. He and I have a special relationship. We like to be together and enjoy each other's company. We used to watch an old black and white western TV drama called "The Rifleman." On the show, Lucas is a single dad raising his son, Mark. As we began watching these shows, I noticed that almost every episode ended with the father and son processing what lessons they had learned during their adventure, and then reconnecting at a deeper level. During these tender closing moments John would often reach over to me and say, "You Lucas and me Mark." This was years ago, but he still brings it up when we meet someone. He will say, "Pop Lucas, me Mark."

The first thing John does when he gets up in the morning is to come and find Papa. He calls me Pop, he calls me Steve, he calls me anything he wants to call me. If I'm still in bed, he crawls in next to me and just snuggles. If I'm in my office, he finds me. If I'm reading my Bible, he'll get out his Bible. He can't read, he doesn't speak clearly, but he wants to do what I am doing, and he thinks I am the cat's meow.

Now, I know my wife would say she loves me unconditionally, and my other sons would say they do as well. But in my thinking, I am convinced if I'm a better guy and read more books on relationships and go to marriage seminars, Sandi will like me more. It's probably not true, but this is how I perceive it.

But there is something unexplainably different about the way Johnny loves and accepts me. He doesn't care how much money I make. He is not impressed by what I do, or how effective of a speaker I am, or whether I have accomplished anything. He just loves me, and I love him. We love each other for who we are and not for what we can or cannot do.

I don't know if this conveys enough of a description of our relationship, but my eyes are watering as I write this even now. The love John and I share is the closest I have come to experiencing unconditional love. One day, I finally articulated what had been going on in my heart and said, "Lord, I'd really like to know you love me like I love Johnny."

The Family is the Building Block

For over 30 years I have been certain the family is the basic building block of the church and society. After creating the world in six days, God created what we know as family. He took one man and one woman, made them one flesh, and told them to be fruitful and multiply. This was before Abraham, before Israel, before Moses and the law. God designed the family. He crafted it. It was His idea.

I have studied the concept of family, designed small group studies for husbands and fathers, written a book about how to have family worship in your home, and made family my top priority in my own home. While I am aware all families are dysfunctional to some degree, I am utterly convinced that if you genuinely want to transform a church or a town, creating more programs is not the answer. Focus on helping families. Healthy families make healthy churches, towns, counties, states, and countries.

As a youth minister, pastor, teacher, and summer camp director, I observed committed families had a greater impact on the positive spiritual development of the children than programs designed to reach youth. Bottom line: You can't replace Mom and Dad.

I know as a Christian husband and father, my primary calling is is to love my wife as Christ loved the church and raise my children in the nurture and admonition of the Lord. When the discussions first began about having a family business I thought I was doing well as a husband and father. Even though I worked hard, my priorities were always intended to be God, family, work/ministry.

In 2009 I was addressing a group of parents at a conference in Alaska. I was speaking about teaching and disciplining your children and quoted Deuteronomy 6:7. "You shall teach them diligently to your children, and shall talk of them when you sit in your house, and when you walk by the way, and when you lie down, and when you rise."

After the session, a mom approached me and asked why I had left out the two preceding verses. I went back and read them. "You shall love the Lord your God with all your heart and with all your soul and with all your might. And these words that I command you today shall be on your heart." (Deuteronomy 6:5-6)

As I read through Deuteronomy 6:5-7 a heavenly light bulb went on for me as I saw the beauty and wisdom of the order in which these verses were given, by inspiration of the Spirit, through Moses. Reading these verses in the proper sequence makes so much sense. Before I can do an effective job teaching my children to love God, I must love God with all my heart, soul, and might. I cannot teach them to love His words, until His words are on my heart. To be able to convey these truths diligently to my children, I must be applying them in my own life. How could I have missed this crucial truth?

As I love God with everything in me, and His words are uppermost in my heart, then and only then, will my love for God and His word spill out when I am talking, sitting, walking, and rising. Discovering this principle prompted me to ask God to revive my heart and help me love Him with all my heart, soul, and might. I wanted to fulfill verse 5 so I could apply verse 7.

Ephesians Misplace Their Priorities

I also knew it was possible for Christians to lose their first love, as in the case of the Ephesian Church in Revelation 2:2-4. "I know your works, your toil and your patient endurance, and how you cannot bear with those who are evil, but have tested those who call themselves apostles and are not, and found them to be false. I know you are enduring patiently and bearing up for my name's sake, and you have not grown weary. But I have this against you, that you have abandoned the love you had at first." I personally don't believe they lost their salvation for they were still the church, but they had misplaced priorities and the fire of their love for God was only a flicker.

Knowing the Ephesian church struggled to maintain their first love, I reread portions of Paul's letter to this same church for more insight into their spiritual condition. It seems they had a problem assimilating grace and the love of God which Paul addressed. In the second chapter I found wonderful verses about unconditional love and the gift of grace.

With Deuteronomy 6 and the Ephesian Church in mind, I began to ask God to renew my love for Him, help me to love Him with all my heart. I also employed an inspired prayer I discovered in Ephesians 3:14-19. "For this reason I bow my knees before the Father, from whom every family in heaven and on earth is named, that according to the riches of His glory He may grant you to be strengthened with power through His Spirit in your inner being, so that Christ may dwell in your hearts through faith—that you, being rooted and grounded in love, may have strength to comprehend with all the saints what is the breadth and length and height and depth, and to know the love of Christ that surpasses knowledge, that you may be filled with all the fullness of God."

Great Commandment

I knew God would answer these prayers because it is His will for His children to love God. It is the first and greatest commandment according to Jesus in Matthew 22:37-38. "You shall love the Lord your God with all your heart and with all your soul and with all your mind. This is the great and first commandment."

When we pray according to His will, He always hears us and answers. "This is the confidence that we have toward Him, that if we ask anything according to His will He hears us. If we know that He hears us in whatever we ask, we know that we have the requests that we have asked of Him." (1 John 5:14-15) I was expecting an answer. I was surprised and pleased at how God began to answer my request.

Prayer

Father work deeply in our hearts. Quicken us by your Spirit to love you with all our heart, soul, mind, and strength. Save us from abandoning the love we had for you at first. Let the love of God be "poured into our hearts through the Holy Spirit who has been given to us," (Romans 5:5) so we will not only know in our heads, but believe in our innermost being, the thoughts and affections you have for each of us as Your adopted children. In the name of Jesus, amen.

Note: In this revised edition, I have added questions to assist in processing the information in each chapter. Work through them for your own study, talk them out with your spouse, or study them in a small group setting, "for where two or three are gathered in my name, there am I among them." (Matthew 18:20) May God bless you on your journey to know the love of God in a deep and richer way.

QUESTIONS FOR REFLECTION

1. What was your salvation encounter with God like? Write a few sentences or a paragraph detailing those moments. Whatever your experience, acknowledge it.

2. Can you identify with Steve's statement, "No matter what I did, I felt driven to do more...I thought I would never quite measure up and kept trying to do more to please Him"? Explain.

3. Why do you think believers struggle so much with thinking that God loves us more if we do more for him? Explain how that idea has manifested itself in your life.

4. Read these verses aloud slowly and thoughtfully: Deuteronomy 6:5-7 aloud slowly and thoughtfully. What do you think God wants to convey to His children here?

5. Read Ephesians 3:14-19, by yourself and/or with others. Ask the Lord to help you love Him with all your heart, soul, mind, and strength. Pray these prayers consistently for a few days, or weeks, or months.

CHAPTER 2: SURPRISED BY GOD'S REALLY GOOD NEWS

Over a period of a year or two I had been prompted to ask God to help me understand His love in my heart of hearts and not just in my head. I was seeking Him to help me believe He loved me unconditionally, as my gifted son loved me. I was asking Him to help me love Him with all my heart, soul, mind, and strength. And I was praying for God to help me grasp the "breadth and length and height and depth, and to know the love of Christ that surpasses knowledge." What I now see in hindsight is these prayers were all to be answered the same way.

In the summer of 2012 I was surprised by how God chose to answer. I expected to awaken one morning with a divine quickening in my breast and find myself loving God and His word with a renewed passion. Instead, He began revealing His love for me, through a variety of scriptures, sermons, songs, and other means. I remonstrated God and said, "This is not what I have been asking. I know you love me, but I want to love you more." Then it dawned on me, this is how God operates. "We love because he first loved us." (1 John 4:19)

I was learning the more I assimilated how much God loved me, the more I loved Him. God always takes the initiative. There are several scriptures revealing this concept. "For while we were still weak, at the right time Christ died for the ungodly. For one will scarcely die for a righteous person— though perhaps for a good person one would dare even to die—but God shows His love for us in that while we were still sinners, Christ died for us." (Romans 5:6-8)

"The Son of Man came to seek and to save the lost." (Luke 19:10) God is the one who seeks us. "He came to his own, and his own people did not receive him." (John 1:11) We would never have asked God to send His son to die for us. We didn't even know we needed Jesus to take our sins upon Himself. We were blind and lost. "But when the fullness of the time came, God sent forth his Son." (Galatians 4:4)

One of the scriptures God used to reveal His love to me was John 15:9. Jesus is speaking to His disciples when He says, "As the Father has loved me, so have I loved you." What was meant by the statement, "As much as God the Father loves His son Jesus, in the same way Jesus loves us"? I stopped to ponder this one verse and while several insights have emerged since this time, at this particular stage in my journey, I received one simple message, Jesus loves me as much as His Dad loves Him.

Jesus is praying for His disciples and for us in John 17:20. "I do not ask for these only, but also for those who will believe in me through their word." In the last verse in this chapter He adds these words, "I made known to them your name, and I will continue to make it known, that the love with which you have loved me may be in them, and I in them." (John 17:27) Jesus is asking God to help us know and posses the same divine love He had received from His Dad.

There is no question God the Father and Jesus the Son have an incredible relationship. They are tight. They are in perfect communion and always have been throughout eternity, except for a brief moment when Jesus was made sin for us. Over one hundred passages speak about the relationship between Jesus and His Dad in the Gospel of John.

Knowing how much His Dad loved Him, Jesus looks at us and says, "As the Father has loved me, so have I loved you."(John 15:9) Those inspired words penetrated my heart, and I began to comprehend how much Jesus loves me, and you.

Even Parents can Learn Something New at Camp

The next step in my journey was understanding the breadth and depth of the gospel. During the summer, my son John and I attended a Joni and Friends family retreat. We had been going to this camp since 2006 and always looked forward to attending. My first trip to camp was when I served as the camp pastor, leading the morning devotions each day. Usually the camp pastor would talk about a subject which had something to do with suffering or hope since everyone at camp has a family member with some form of disability.

This summer proved to be different, and I was pleasantly surprised and wonderfully edified. The first morning we met, the pastor announced he would be speaking on the gospel. He was true to his word, and for the next three mornings he expounded on one verse, 2 Corinthians 5:21. "For our sake he made Him to be sin who knew no sin, so that in Him we might become the righteousness of God."

The primary insight I received was about the gift of righteousness. I had known forgiveness was a gift from God, but as he explained this single verse in detail, I saw that "In Him I might become the righteousness of God." Forgiveness and righteousness are both free gifts of God. Jesus paid the price and we receive the benefit.

When I asked Jesus to forgive my sins in the summer of 1968, He did. I mistakenly believed this gave me a clean slate and it was now up to me, to build and extend the Kingdom of God. I had known of the robes of Christ which cover us in such a way that as God sees us, He sees Jesus, but I had never grasped the breadth of this idea. In Christ, we have become the righteousness of God. When I saw this truth, I knew I didn't have to do anything to please God, I was already pleasing to Him because I was in Christ. He had done it all. I breathed a deep sigh of relief in my spirit when I heard this scripture explained. I gained other insights from the teaching, but this was the most important insight to me.

"For our sake he made Him to be sin who knew no sin, so that in Him we might become the righteousness of God." (2 Corinthians 5:21)

There is so much with in this one verse, the first three words are often overlooked. "For our sake," sets the stage for the whole passage. God loves us and this is His motivation for enduring the agony of the crucifixion. I hope I never lose the wonder of God creating us, knowing us, and loving us. He desires our fellowship. "For our sake."

He "made Him to be sin who knew no sin." I knew only Jesus could take away our sin since He had no sins of His own. He was the spotless lamb being sacrificed for our sins. What I grasped in a deeper way, was the price the Father and the Son paid for Jesus becoming sin.

Sin separates us from God. "Your iniquities have made the separation between you and your God." (Isaiah 59:2) In the garden of Eden, when Adam and Eve disobeyed God and ate the forbidden fruit, they knew they were naked. They then hid themselves and tried to cover their nakedness with fig leaves. This is the effect of sin.

We all know the feeling of being alone, ashamed, naked, and wanting to cover ourselves, because we have all sinned. Sin is common to man. Conviction of sin is an awful universal sensation. When I first heard the gospel, the knowledge I could be forgiven was very attractive. I wanted a clean slate. I had been a boy who was usually in some sort of trouble and the thought of having a fresh start resonated with my 14-year old heart.

I am generally pretty quick to extend forgiveness when someone sins against me, for I have tasted separation and conviction and I don't like it. Conviction is unpleasant and distasteful. I have been convicted many times and subsequently had to ask forgiveness of God and others. Sin and its effects are not pleasant.

Jesus had never known sin, conviction, or separation, for He had never sinned. The pastor commented there was probably no one more unprepared or ill equipped to be made sin than Jesus. I hope you will think about this statement. The unique sinlessness of Jesus which made Him the only one qualified to bear our sin, also made Him the only one who had never tasted the fruit of sin, separation from our Holy God.

Consider how close and intimate the Father was with His Son. They had enjoyed uninterrupted harmony for eternity. Perhaps reading this portion of Proverbs will help you get a glimpse of their unique relationship. They describe creation from the perspective of Wisdom interacting with the Creator. I see Wisdom as Jesus, and the Creator being the Father. These scriptures may or may not refer to Jesus and the Father, but they portray two people who were daily each other's delight which is certainly an accurate depiction of our God and His only begotten Son.

"The LORD possessed me at the beginning of His work, the first of His acts of old. Ages ago I was set up, at the first, before the beginning of the earth. When there were no depths I was brought forth, when there were no springs abounding with water. Before the mountains had been shaped, before the hills, I was brought forth, before He had made the earth with its fields, or the first of the dust of the world. When He established the heavens, I was there; when He drew a circle on the face of the deep, when He made firm the skies above, when He established the fountains of the deep, when He assigned to the sea its limit, so that the waters might not transgress His command, when He marked out the foundations of the earth, then I was beside Him, like a master workman, and I was daily His delight, rejoicing before Him always, rejoicing in His inhabited world and delighting in the children of man." (Proverbs 8:22–31)

When Jesus became sin on the cross, darkness descended. These two kindred spirits, who had been one since before time and only experienced perfect love, harmony, and connection, were now separated because of our collective sin. Jesus was alone, for the first time, ever. The Father turned away, because of our sin, for the only time, ever.

The most painful phrase ever uttered, and one which breaks my heart because it broke His heart, is "My God, my God, why have you forsaken me?" (Matthew 27:46) The sinless, immaculate, all loving, all righteous Father had to turn His back on His precious Son because He was made sin, our sin.

Some scholars surmise this heart rending cry was heard echoing from one end of eternity to the other. Scripture supports this conclusion for "As far as the east is from the west, so far does He remove our transgressions from us." (Psalm 103:12)

Just as I cannot fathom the love they shared, I also am not able to comprehend the pain of their separation. They, Father and Son, endured this agony for us. They paid the highest price so we might have our sins removed and be in fellowship with them. "I do not ask for these only, but also for those who will believe in me through their word, that they may all be one, just as you, Father, are in me, and I in you, that they also may be in us." (John 17:20-21)

As I type these words, I am in reverent awe and want to be still. This truism alone is enough to inspire eternal worship. He took our sins and tasted the desperate separation and fruit of sin, for us. But there is more good news in the second half of the verse, "that in Him we might become the righteousness of God."

When our speaker began to think through each word in this phrase he had a white board on a stand brought to the front of the room and asked the audience to help brainstorm. We attempted to document the righteous acts of Jesus on earth. He cast out demons, healed the sick, raised the dead, fed the multitudes, cleansed lepers, preached words of life, died for our sins, prayed for us, blessed children, and forgave the woman taken in adultery. "There are also many other things that Jesus did. Were every one of them to be written, I suppose that the world itself could not contain the books that would be written." (John 21:25)

The second part of 2 Corinthians 5:21 reads, "so that in Him we might become the righteousness of God." Because He was made sin for us, we receive forgiveness as He takes our sin upon Himself. These two words "in Him" make us know we also have become the righteousness of God. His righteousness has been attributed to us.

I knew this concept of imputed righteousness in part, but when we specifically rehearsed the righteousness of Jesus and all of His righteous deeds, I was able to grasp this truth in a new way.

When we receive the gift of God, eternal life and forgiveness of sins, and choose to follow Jesus in baptism, scripture teaches we are "in Him" and "in Christ." (Philippians 3:9, Galatians 3:26) When baptized we are "baptized into His death." (Romans 6:3) According to Colossians 3:3, "You have died, and your life is hidden with Christ in God."

In Christ, we have become the righteousness of God. Not only is forgiveness from sin a gift of God, so also is the righteousness of Christ a gift as well. All of the righteous acts of Jesus have been credited to our account. When God looks at us, He sees on our record, that we cast out demons, raised the dead, healed the sick, and fed the multitude.

It helps me to think of this crediting of accounts with a bank illustration. Let's imagine I receive a monthly statement that says I have a debt the size of the U.S. government. My first thought is the bank has made a mistake, but when I call to check, the numbers are accurate. I am then filled with a sense of hopelessness as there is no possible way I could ever pay off this debt.

The next statement comes and shows someone named J. Christ has paid my debt, and I now have a zero balance. The relief I experience is indescribable and worthy of my thanks for eternity. A chorus I learned years ago by Ellis J. Crum describes my gratitude:

> He paid a debt He did not owe. I owed a debt I could not pay,
>
> I needed someone to wash my sins away.
>
> And now I sing a brand new song,
> "Amazing Grace,"
>
> Christ Jesus paid a debt that I could never pay.

As happy as I now am with a zero balance, I almost don't want to open the next bank statement when it arrives but when I do, I find there has been a large amount of funds deposited. The depositor was also someone named J. Christ, and it says all of His assets have been transferred into my account. I am speechless.

This is what it means to receive the gift of forgiveness as well as the gift of righteousness. If you need a little more convincing, consider these scriptures from Paul's epistle to the Romans.

"It was credited to Him as righteousness. Now, not for His sake only was it written that it was credited to Him but for our sake also to Him what we'll be credited as those who believe in Him who raised Jesus our Lord from the dead." (Romans 4:22)

"For if, because of one man's trespass, death reigned through that one man, much more will those who receive the abundance of grace and the free gift of righteousness reign in life through the one man Jesus Christ." (Romans 5:17)

Again in Philippians 3:8-9, "Indeed, I count everything as loss because of the surpassing worth of knowing Christ Jesus my Lord. For His sake I have suffered the loss of all things and count them as rubbish, in order that I may gain Christ and be found in Him, not having a righteousness of my own that comes from the law, but that which comes through faith in Christ, the righteousness from God that depends on faith."

Perhaps this is old news to you but this was new news for me. I had mistakenly believed righteousness was something I do, and not something that Jesus already did.

Prayer

"For this reason, because I have heard of your faith in the Lord Jesus and your love toward all the saints, I do not cease to give thanks for you, remembering you in my prayers, that the God of our Lord Jesus Christ, the Father of glory, may give you the Spirit of wisdom and of revelation in the knowledge of him, having the eyes of your hearts enlightened, that you may know what is the hope to which he has called you, what are the riches of his glorious inheritance in the saints, and what is the immeasurable greatness of his power toward us who believe" (Ephesians 1:15-19)

QUESTIONS FOR REFLECTION

1. There are an abundance of scripture passages in this section. Which one(s) did the Spirit impress on your heart? Write out or meditate on this truth for a few days.

2. This chapter emphasizes righteousness as God's gift to you: "in Christ, we have become the righteousness of God." Picture two contrasting images. One person is saved and focuses on doing everything possible to please God, and prays, "What can I do for you today?" The other person is also saved, and rejoices every morning, "God, You have made me righteous and You like me! Help me love You and share Your Love." With which person do you most identify?

3. Meditate on the phrase Jesus cried out on the cross, "My God, my God, why have you forsaken me?" Try to put yourself in Jesus' sandals, and feel what it must have been like to be separated from his Dad, close-knit as their relationship was.

4. Think and about what it means that "You have died, and your life is hidden with Christ in God." Jot a list of the righteous acts that Jesus did here on earth and how they apply to you, since your life is hidden with Christ in God. Discuss it with your group.

5. Is the message of this chapter, "righteousness from God that depends on faith," old news to you, or new news? Explain how.

CHAPTER 3:
AS THE FATHER
LOVED THE SON

I used to read quickly over the first part of John 15:9, "As the Father has loved me, so have I loved you. Now remain in my love." I have since seen a special nugget of truth hidden there. The strength of the statement "Jesus loves us" is based on how the Father loved the Son. The little word "as" speaks volumes. Just as the Father loved the Son, so too did the Son love us. How did the Father love the Son? What transpired over the first thirty years of the life of our Savior?

Jesus had a relatively short run as a public figure. Most of His life was spent in the home of Joseph and Mary, surrounded by his siblings. These may have been the most important years of His life. For this time of preparation enabled Him to live a sinless life, withstand the temptations of the devil, expose the hypocrisy of the religious establishment, and train a group of men and women to change the world.

We only have a few glimpses of these formative years. The son of Joseph went to the feasts in Jerusalem. "When the feast was ended, as they were returning, the boy Jesus stayed behind in Jerusalem. His parents did not know it, but supposing Him to be in the group they went a day's journey, but then they began to search for Him among their relatives and acquaintances, and when they did not find Him, they returned to Jerusalem, searching for Him. After three days they found Him in the temple, sitting among the teachers, listening to them and asking them questions. And all who heard Him were amazed at His understanding and His answers." (Luke 2:43-47)

Maybe Jesus was born with a halo, and had a perfect and complete understanding of the Bible from the womb, but I think He had to learn and meditate on the word of God. "Though he was a Son, yet learned obedience by the things which he suffered." (Hebrews 5:8) This passage shows us Jesus learned to obey.

That He was well-versed in the truth is documented in several places. I have chosen only a few examples. It was His custom to read the scrolls and He was familiar with them. I would love to have been a fly on the wall when He read the scriptures in the synagogue. "He came to Nazareth, where He had been brought up: and He entered, as His custom was, into the synagogue on the sabbath day, and stood up to read. And there was delivered unto Him the book of the prophet Isaiah. And He opened the book, and found the place where it was written." (Luke 4:16-17)

One of the greatest Bible studies ever conducted was on the road to Emmaus. Jesus was the teacher, while Cleopas and a friend, were the students. "Beginning with Moses and all the Prophets, He interpreted to them in all the Scriptures the things concerning Himself." (Luke 24:27)

He affirmed the law in the Sermon on the Mount. "Do not think that I have come to abolish the Law or the Prophets; I have not come to abolish them but to fulfill them. For truly, I say to you, until heaven and earth pass away, not an iota, not a dot, will pass from the Law until all is accomplished." (Matthew 5:17-18) Five times in this chapter He says, "You have heard that it was said" and proceeds to give the correct interpretation of the verse. For example, "You have heard that it was said, 'You shall love your neighbor and hate your enemy.' But I say to you, Love your enemies and pray for those who persecute you." (Matthew 5:43-44)

When He was tempted by the devil he responded by quoting scripture from Deuteronomy. "The devil said to him, 'If you are the Son of God, command this stone to become bread.' And Jesus answered him, "It is written, 'Man shall not live by bread alone.'" (Luke 4:3-4)

The primary reason I mention the formative years of the life of Jesus, is because it was during this time Jesus and His Father became acquainted. They had known each other while in heaven, for eternity. No one knows how much of this time He recalled after being born as a baby and learning to walk, talk, eat, and obey His parents. But based on what we have already seen, He did learn important truths while living in the bosom of His family. In addition to learning the word of God, "As the Father has loved me," makes me think He also learned to experience the love of God.

In the Gospels there are more than one hundred references which speak of the relationship between Jesus and His Father. I have selected a few passages to give you a sense of these verses. More complete lists are found in Appendix A and Appendix B.

At His baptism Jesus was verbally affirmed by His Dad.

"When Jesus was baptized, immediately He went up from the water, and behold, the heavens were opened to Him, and he saw the Spirit of God descending like a dove and coming to rest on Him; and behold, a voice from heaven said, 'This is my beloved Son, with whom I am well pleased.'" (Matthew 3:16–17)

The Father encouraged His Son in the presence of His disciples.

"Behold, a bright cloud overshadowed them, and a voice from the cloud said, 'This is my beloved Son, with whom I am well pleased; listen to Him.'" (Matthew 17:5)

He always hears His Son's prayers.

"So they took away the stone. And Jesus lifted up his eyes and said, 'Father, I thank you that you have heard me. I knew that you always hear me.'" (John 11:41–42)

The Father taught the Son.

"Jesus said to them, 'When you have lifted up the Son of Man, then you will know that I am he, and that I do nothing on my own authority, but speak just as the Father taught me.'" (John 8:28)

The Son depended on His Dad.

"Truly, truly, I say to you, the Son can do nothing of His own accord, but only what He sees the Father doing. For whatever the Father does, that the Son does likewise. For the Father loves the Son and shows Him all that he himself is doing." (John 5:19-20)

They are always together.

"He who sent me is with me. He has not left me alone, for I always do the things that are pleasing to Him." (John 8:29)

His Dad has His back.

Jesus answered, "If I glorify myself, my glory is nothing. It is my Father who glorifies me." (John 8:54)

They are in complete harmony.

"I and the Father are one." (John 10:30)

The Father trusts His Son.

"The Father loves the Son and has given all things into His hand." (John 3:35)

Jesus asks the Father to include us in Their intimate communion.

"I do not ask for these only, but also for those who will believe in me through their word, that they may all be one, just as you, Father, are in me, and I in you, that they also may be in us, so

that the world may believe that you have sent me."
(John 17:20-21)

Jesus was loved perfectly. I am sure Mary and
Joseph were Godly parents, but the Father in heaven
was a perfect Dad. "Every good gift and every perfect
gift is from above, coming down from the Father of
lights with whom there is no variation or shadow
due to change." (James 1:17) God is love. Everything
which is good and perfect comes from God. Perfect
love comes from above, from God Himself. God first
loves Jesus, then Jesus loves us, but love begins with
God the Father. Whether the sending of His Son, or
the sending of the Holy Spirit, all good things come
from God who is above.

There were probably a lot of early morning walks
along the Sea of Galilee, or quiet evenings spent
on a lonely hillside, where the Father and the Son
communed. We don't know how this relationship
was built and nurtured, but it was the plan of God
for Jesus to devote thirty years preparing to fulfill
His brief, but eternally effective earthly ministry.

Prayer

Thank you for loving us just as you loved your
only begotten Son. Thank you for taking the initiative
and in love, sending Jesus to die for us. Anoint our
mind and spirit to assimilate and apprehend in a
new and living way how much you care for each of
us. In the name of your Beloved Son Jesus, amen
I am learning to discern the condition of my own
spirit and heart, and speak accordingly.

QUESTIONS FOR REFLECTION

1. "Of the references made by Jesus to His Father, listed in this chapter and Appendix A, which are most meaningful to you? Rewrite them in your own words, paraphrasing them. Consider looking them up on www.biblegateway. com and copy several other translations or paraphrases of the same verse(s).

2. Think about your relationship to your Heavenly Father. Do the things mentioned in these verses pertain to you and God?"

3. Ponder how you relate to your earthly father. Has your relationship with your dad influenced how you relate to God as your Father?

4. "There were probably a lot of early morning walks along the Sea of Galilee, or quiet evenings spent on a lonely hillside, where the Father and the Son communed." How and where do you make space for communing with God?

5. Consider asking God to give you an idea for how to establish one. Ask Him to give you a hunger and desire to be still and wait on the Lord, pouring out your heart to Him, and listening to Him.

CHAPTER 4: IDENTITY

Jesus was the most grounded person who walked this earth. When the Son of God graduated with honors from the training God uniquely designed for Him, He headed to the Jordan River to be baptized by John. After He emerged from the water, He was given the best presents any graduate could receive, a divine accolade from His Father, and the gift of the Holy Spirit. God affirmed for all the world to hear that this was His boy, and He was pleased with Him.

"When Jesus was baptized, immediately He went up from the water, and behold, the heavens were opened to Him, and he saw the Spirit of God descending like a dove and coming to rest on Him; and behold, a voice from heaven said, 'This is my beloved Son, with whom I am well pleased.'" (Matthew 3:16–17)

The training period was over and He was ready to begin His ministry. He had the blessing of His Dad and the presence of the Holy Spirit. But first He was led into the wilderness for forty days and nights of fasting. At the end of this time of testing, He went from feeling on top of the world to being vulnerable. Not having eaten for over a month, the devil attacked Him at the point where He was most susceptible. When we read this account, we see hunger and bread, but notice the first words out of the liar's mouth. "If you are the Son of God." (Matthew 4:3)

"Then Jesus was led up by the Spirit into the wilderness to be tempted by the devil. And after fasting forty days and forty nights, He was hungry. And the tempter came and said to him, 'If you are the Son of God, command these stones to become loaves of bread.'" (Matthew 4:1-3)

Our arch enemy knows where to strike. The real battle was not his appetite but his identity. God the Father had just told Jesus in a voice from heaven, "This is my beloved Son," and now the deceiver was implying He wasn't. It was a subtle and deadly ploy. Jesus successfully resisted the temptation by employing the sword of the Spirit, the word of God. "It is written, 'Man shall not live by bread alone, but by every word that comes from the mouth of God.'" (Matthew 4:4)

Jesus successfully warded off two more temptations and the devil left Him alone. Jesus knew who He was. He was the Son of God, the Messiah.

Jesus was tested further when he returned to His home country. When Luke sets out to write an accurate account of the life and ministry of Jesus, he moves from the temptation in the wilderness to the town of Nazareth in Galilee. "When the devil had ended every temptation, he departed from Him until an opportune time. And Jesus returned in the power of the Spirit to Galilee, and a report about Him went out through all the surrounding country. And He taught in their synagogues, being glorified by all. And He came to Nazareth, where He had been brought up." (Luke 4:13-16)

Then, as He always did, He read the scripture to all who were gathered that Sabbath. "And as was His custom, he went to the synagogue on the Sabbath day, and He stood up to read. And the scroll of the prophet Isaiah was given to Him. He unrolled the scroll and found the place where it was written, 'The Spirit of the Lord is upon me, because He has anointed me to proclaim good news to the poor. He has sent me to proclaim liberty to the captives and recovering of sight to the blind, to set at liberty those who are oppressed, to proclaim the year of the Lord's favor.'" (Luke 4:16-19)

I imagine a hush came over the people as He "rolled up the scroll and gave it back to the attendant and sat down. And the eyes of all in the synagogue were fixed on Him. And he began to say to them, 'Today this Scripture has been fulfilled in your hearing.' And all spoke well of Him and marveled at the gracious words that were coming from His mouth. And they said, 'Is not this Joseph's son?'" (Luke 4:20-22)

This took place in Nazareth, his hometown, where everyone knew Him and His family and where "no prophet is acceptable." (Luke 4:24) This is the toughest place to begin a ministry. But Jesus was rooted and grounded in the knowledge that He was the Son of God. He knew, even if they didn't, who God said He was. He did not need their affirmation nor their encouragement. They marveled at His words and His repose, but whether they believed in Him or not, He knew who He was down deep in the core of His being.

Born Again-Again

This pattern of becoming a child of God and then having our identity as sons and daughters of God questioned or tested is replicated in the life of believers who have been born from above. At the baptism of Jesus, the heavens opened, the Spirit descended on Him, words of identity and affirmation were uttered, "This is my beloved Son in whom I am well pleased." (Matthew 3:16-17)

In a similar way, when we are born from above, we see or understand the kingdom for the first time, and the Spirit leads us to confess that Jesus is Lord. The same Spirit witnesses with our spirit that we are children of God, deeply loved by our Dad. We discover we are well-pleasing, for we are no longer enemies of God, but have been thoroughly forgiven and declared "righteous" in Christ.

I believe I became an adopted child of God when I first asked Jesus to forgive my sins and come into my heart. But these past few years God has made me know afresh I am His son, I am beloved, and He is pleased with me. I also know I have to fight to hold on to my new identity in Christ, just as Jesus contended with the devil about His own identity as the Son of God.

Our Temptation is Common to Man

The enemy of our souls is the same as the enemy of our master, and he knows where we are susceptible. When guilt and condemnation are no longer effective, he attacks our identity and who we are in Christ, by casting doubt on whether we are truly children of God. Just as Jesus responded to these barbs from hell with the sword of the Spirit, the word of God, we too need to quote scripture to combat the same accusation. If you need more ammunition to ward off the attacks of the deceiver, consider this powerful passage from the book of Romans:

"For all who are led by the Spirit of God are sons of God. For you did not receive the spirit of slavery to fall back into fear, but you have received the Spirit of adoption as sons, by whom we cry, 'Abba! Father!' The Spirit Himself bears witness with our spirit that we are children of God, and if children, then heirs— heirs of God and fellow heirs with Christ."
(Romans 8:14–17)

God has sent His Spirit to communicate with our Spirit that we are children of God. We are His kids, His beloved children. No matter how we feel; or what we have done; or how much time we have spent praying or reading the word; or what kind of spouse or parent we have been today; we belong to Him. He is our Dad. Our Abba Daddy.

If you need more ammunition to ward off the stench of the deceiver, consider this powerful affirmation of God being for us!

"Those whom He foreknew He also predestined to be conformed to the image of His Son, in order that He might be the firstborn among many brothers. And those whom He predestined He also called, and those whom He called He also justified, and those whom He justified He also glorified.

What then shall we say to these things? If God is for us, who can be against us? He who did not spare His own Son but gave Him up for us all, how will He not also with Him graciously give us all things? Who shall bring any charge against God's elect? It is God who justifies. Who is to condemn? Christ Jesus is the one who died—more than that, who was raised—who is at the right hand of God, who indeed is interceding for us. Who shall separate us from the love of Christ? Shall tribulation, or distress, or persecution, or famine, or nakedness, or danger, or sword? As it is written, 'For your sake we are being killed all the day long; we are regarded as sheep to be slaughtered.'

No, in all these things we are more than conquerors through Him who loved us. For I am sure that neither death nor life, nor angels nor rulers, nor things present nor things to come, nor powers, nor height nor depth, nor anything else in all creation, will be able to separate us from the love of God in Christ Jesus our Lord." (Romans 8:29–39)

Adopted Children of God

Knowing we are children of God is our birthright and our identity in Christ. It is not simply another edifying truth, but central to who we are and whose we are. I was battling a temptation recently and wondering what I would do if placed in a compromising situation. I sensed God communicate to my spirit to not yield because, "thou art my son!" I was blessed and strengthened by this powerful affirmation. For I am in Christ, and have been adopted into the family of God, I am indeed a child of God and have taken on the persona and characteristics of my savior and my Dad.

We have been born from above. We have been grafted into the family of God. He is our Dad. Knowing this in the marrow of our being transforms and purifies us. "See what kind of love the Father has given to us, that we should be called children of God; and so we are. The reason why the world does not know us is that it did not know Him. Beloved, we are God's children now, and what we will be has not yet appeared; but we know that when He appears we shall be like Him, because we shall see Him as He is. And everyone who thus hopes in Him purifies himself as He is pure." (1 John 3:1-3)

"When the fullness of time had come, God sent forth His Son, born of woman, born under the law, to redeem those who were under the law, so that we might receive adoption as sons. And because you are sons, God has sent the Spirit of His Son into our hearts, crying, 'Abba! Father!' So you are no longer a slave, but a son, and if a son, then an heir through God." (Galatians 4:4-7) We may feel like we would be content to simply be a servant of God, but God has called us and given us the witness in our hearts that we are His kids.

"To all who did receive him, who believed in his name, he gave the right to become children of God, who were born, not of blood nor of the will of the flesh nor of the will of man, but of God." (John 1:12-13)

Prayer

May God's Good Spirit witness with our spirit that we who have been born from above are truly children of God. May He write these truths on our heart, so we might know beyond a shadow of a doubt, we are His and He is ours. In the name of our Brother Jesus, amen. (Matthew 12:49, 2 Corinthians 3:3)

QUESTIONS FOR REFLECTION

1. How did Satan attack Jesus' identity, and how did Jesus win against his enemy's lies?

2. Knowing your identity in Christ is a crucial part of fulfilling God's purpose for you on earth. Therefore, Satan will do everything he can to bring doubt and uncertainty to your identity in your mind and heart. How do you combat the enemy's lies, according to this chapter?

3. Do you have a favorite verse or verses? Write them on notecards and consider posting them on your mirror

4. Which passages would you like to have memorized so you could effectively wield the sword of the Spirit?

5. "You are no longer a slave, but a son..." Think about the differences between a slave (or servant) and a son. What sets them apart? List some ways. How do those differences apply to YOUR relationship with your Heavenly Dad? How do some ways you behave fit into the "slave" category? The "son" category?

CHAPTER 5:
INSPIRED
ILLUMINATIONS

You are about to read about two very specific times when God wonderfully met me: first in my car, and then in my kitchen. These occurrences were precious and extraordinary. Since then, I have had several similar experiences with the living God. These were times when God revealed himself or some aspect of truth to my heart in a way which was unlike anything I had known or tasted heretofore. When speaking with the Samaritan women at the well Jesus said, "God is spirit, and those who worship him must worship in spirit and truth." (John 4:24)

I believe any dream, vision, or revelation God brings to us should be examined and found to be consistent with the inspired word of God. I have decided to call these precious times "illuminations" because each of these divine communications have illuminated scriptural truths to me. I share them with you in the hope they will encourage you as much as they have helped me.

Perhaps God knew I would need extra help and grace going into a critical time in my life, and He gave me this special dispensation to carry me through a rough patch. Whether He sovereignly intervened in my life with these illuminations, or if He was answering the prayers of my faithful brothers and sisters in Christ or cries from my own desperate, these divine encounters encouraged and sustained me through difficult times. In Psalm 46:1 we read, "God is our refuge and strength, a very present help in trouble." He was certainly a very present help when I was in trouble!

Not only did these experiences illuminate scriptural truths, they revealed God Himself to me in a marked way. I didn't simply learn more about God, I was enabled to know the living God Himself. His character and nature were revealed. I am struggling to put this into words, but I was meeting and interacting with the person of God. As you read these accounts of precious times I have experienced, I hope you will be edified by the truths which are illuminated and the good God we serve and love will also be revealed.

In the Car

It was a particularly difficult family board meeting. After some painful deliberations and a vote, I felt as though I had just lost my family, my business, and my ministry in a half hour. I was alone, lost, and without a compass. My world as I knew it had just been shattered. I left the meeting room and stood in the next room leaning up against a large window sobbing from depths I did not know I possessed. I was suffering from the worst pain I had ever experienced.

Two of my sons saw my agony and came to hold me, but I put up my hand to keep from embracing me. I didn't know where the pain emanated from nor did I know why I resisted their efforts to comfort me. The following January as I was reading in Genesis, I noticed the account of Jacob receiving news that Joseph was dead. I found comfort seeing Jacob's response when in similar straits. "All his sons and all his daughters rose up to comfort him, but he refused to be comforted." (Genesis 37:35)

As I stood staring out the window trying to find some equilibrium. Finally, I was able to gather myself and I walked to my car. It was there I was able to pray, "Oh God, help." I sat gazing heavenward and saw God looking at me. As I sensed his eyes upon me, this verse went through my mind: "To this man will I look, he that is of a poor and contrite spirit and that trembles at my word." (Isaiah 66:2)

God met me in the car and His presence and personalized attention were never needed more. I didn't feel anything for I was numb. But knowing He was looking at me was reassuring. He was still on His throne and He cared. For that afternoon in April was the beginning of the hardest, and in retrospect, the best year of my life.

In the Kitchen

A few months later, on a beautiful Sunday in July, I reached one of the lowest points of my life. I was unable to encourage myself in the Lord. Regardless of what scriptures I read or uplifting music I listened to, I was in the slough of despond. I had been trying to fight this battle by myself for several months and this day I finally ran out of gas.

While I was in this dark place, I sent out an email to thirty friends asking for help. These brothers and sisters in Christ began to pray and reach out to support and encourage me.

Perhaps what happened two days later on Tuesday morning was an answer to the prayers of my support team, or maybe God sovereignly knew this was the right time. Whereas Sunday was the nadir of the summer, Tuesday morning was the beginning of my healing and recovery.

That morning I was feeling pretty good. I had just finished a hearty breakfast, was listening to uplifting Christian music, and reading a book for Christians exploring the biblical roots of the Twelve Step Approach. I was standing in the middle of the kitchen, when I sensed Jesus was standing next to me. He communicated one sentence to my spirit which changed the way I viewed my relationship with Him. The specific words belong to only me, but I can share that in that one sentence He made me know He made me, He knew me, and He formed me in my mother's womb. I had been designed to do what I do, and He liked me just the way I was. I began to laugh out loud.

I had been feeling so worthless I was wondering if I needed a personality transplant or perhaps should reinvent myself. But in one phrase, He affirmed my identity and personality, built me up, joked with me, and conveyed His pleasure in me. This was the first of several encounters I had with Spirit of the living God that summer. I still am amazed at how He could pack so much important information in one sentence, but He is God and He knows me, and He knew just what I needed to hear. For He is the one who created me, made me in His image, and formed me in my mother's womb.

"For you formed my inward parts; you knitted me together in my mother's womb. My frame was not hidden from you, when I was being made in secret, Your eyes saw my unformed substance; in your book were written, every one of them, the days that were formed for me, when as yet there was none of them. How precious to me are your thoughts, O God! How vast is the sum of them! If I would count them, they are more than the sand. I awake, and I am still with you." (Psalms 139:13–17)

Further Illuminations: No Baggage

Even after this wonderful visitation by the Spirit of Jesus in the kitchen, I still had to seek God daily. One morning I awakened and God seemed like He was a million miles away. My first thought was I should find one of the studies I had made about how God never leaves us or forsakes us, or something similar. I considered playing some good music and worshiping God while I read my Bible, but I didn't have the energy. Instead I said out loud, "Do you still love me as much today as you did yesterday?" I wasn't feeling very reverent or respectful, and simply didn't have the energy to seek God.

God graciously answered my request by giving me a picture. I saw Jesus standing on the clouds with blue sky all around and His arms spread wide. He was laughing when He said, "Of course I do, I don't have any baggage."

As soon as I saw this image, several scriptures came zipping through my mind to confirm this image was indeed from God.

God is light.

"God is light, and in him is no darkness at all." (1 John 1:5)

God is love, all the time. He is not loving, He is love.

"God is love, and whoever abides in love abides in God, and God abides in him." (1 John 4:16)

God never changes. He is.

"For I the Lord do not change." (Malachi 3:6)

"Jesus Christ is the same yesterday and today and forever." (Hebrews 13:8)

We have this treasure in earthen vessels. In other words we are earthy, cracked pots. We are susceptible to changes in weather, our emotions, how much sleep we have had, and whether we have eaten a good breakfast. We are fragile creatures dependent on many variables. God however, is always light, always loving. He never changes. He is the great unchangeable I Am. I appreciate this picture of Jesus standing with the clouds at His feet because it reminds me of flying on a commercial airline. On the ground, it can be cold, windy, gray, and raining, but when you get high enough, the jet breaks through the clouds, and all is light. It is God's country where all is light.

We are given a picture of life in this world in Revelation 21:22-23. "I saw no temple in the city, for its temple is the Lord God the Almighty and the Lamb. And the city has no need of sun or moon to shine on it, for the glory of God gives it light, and its lamp is the Lamb."

The expression, "I don't have any baggage," is important because only God doesn't have any personal issues. However, we each have scars and hurts from our past. Nobody likes to readily acknowledge our own stuff because it hurts, so we guard ourselves, our woundedness, and our brokenness. I asked God once why I liked some people easily, and others I had to work at being able to love. He made me know it is our own pain which hinders us from loving and connecting with others.

If we really knew and understood people and could see past their defenses and weren't afraid to acknowledge our own issues, we could love everybody. Even though we all share in being broken to some degree, hiding and protecting our own issues reacts with the baggage of others and keeps us from loving our neighbor as ourself.

I think of this special experience frequently because part of my baggage is that I have trouble believing that God likes me and is always smiling when I approach Him in prayer. I struggle with seeing God as the father of the prodigal son always standing in the street with arms spread wide seeking to embrace me when I draw near to Him. Even though this is the image scripture conveys to my mind, I have had trouble believing it applied to me.

Prior to 2012, if you had asked me how I knew that God loved me, I may have responded that God loves the world, and I am a part of the world, therefore God loves me. Or I might have reasoned that it is God's duty to love me, for God is love. But thanks to God moving by His Spirit I am discovering that it is God's pleasure and delight to love me and that He affectionately likes me, and that is good news indeed.

These truths are sinking into my heart and becoming a part of me. Now when I lie in bed processing the day, or when I first awake, I think of my Dad standing there with His arms wide open, smiling, laughing, and happy to see me and hear what is on my heart. God is good, all the time, in every way, and He loves His children to pieces, all the time.

I Miss You Too

A few summers ago I was speaking at a family camp over the Labor Day weekend. That Sunday morning I had been teaching about the most painful part of the crucifixion, Jesus uttering these words out of abandoned agony, "My God, My God why have you forsaken me?"

I know the nails and the physical torment of hanging on a cross must come with incredible pain. But I think the hardest part for Jesus was being separated from His Father for the first time in eternity. Father and Son had been one since before time. They loved each other completely, thoroughly, and fully. They had never been anything but one, in spirit and mind. Theirs was, and is, the perfect relationship.

"For our sake He made Him to be sin who knew no sin, so that in Him we might become the righteousness of God." Jesus, the pure lamb, the sinless Son of God, became sin, for our sake. Sin brings separation. "Your iniquities have made a separation between you and your God, and your sins have hidden His face from you so that He does not hear." (Isaiah 59:2)

Our sin caused Jesus to suffer in a new way. While He was uniquely prepared to bear our sin, He was emotionally ill-equipped to experience His Father turning His back and not hearing His cry. As humans we all know too well what it feels like to have sin impact our relationships with each other and our God. But not Jesus. He had never sinned. He had never been estranged. He and the Father were always one.

Later that Sunday afternoon, I was preparing for the evening session and contemplating the price Jesus paid for bearing my sin. I was also remembering the many times when I had sinned and felt separated from God. During these times I missed

God and His presence. As I was walking across a grassy lawn below the chapel, God whispered to my heart, "I miss you too."

I stopped and my eyes began to fill with tears of gratitude and appreciation as these words sunk into my heart. God loves me so much that when I sin, He misses me. Our Dad likes to be with us and enjoy our fellowship. God really does like His children. Our relationship with our Heavenly Father goes both ways. We love Him and He loves us. Without Jesus bearing our sin, we could not know the joy of being in harmony with our Dad.

A Stone House

One wintry day, I was driving through Chadds Ford, Pennsylvania, on the way to the Philadelphia Airport for a flight to Vermont. On my left was a beautiful stone house made of grey granite. It was also for sale. I would estimate that it was built in the 1700s or 1800s, and I thought it was gorgeous. I really like granite houses and when I saw this one, it struck a deep chord in my heart. There are not many things that I would like to have, but I had a strong desire to have this house or one like it.

I started scheming in my mind how I could afford to purchase it and reasoned since I was approaching retirement age maybe I could sell our current house and buy this one. I considered a home equity loan and almost turned around to get a better look at it and write down the real estate information. All of these thoughts took just a few seconds, when it occurred to me, talk to God about this yearning.

God had continued to be near whenever I approached Him in prayer so I asked Him, "Why do I like stone houses so much?" As soon as I verbalized this prayer, God communicated to me, "I'm building one for you, and I know you better than you know yourself and it is going to be awesome." The thought that I received was that God was the divine architect and since He knew what I really wanted in a home, He was designing one to fit my unique specifications. He was building it and even though I didn't fully know what I wanted in a house, He did.

He also made me know He was joyfully looking forward to showing it to me when I got to heaven. Several scriptures came to mind.

He knows me better than I know myself.

"O Lord, you have searched me and known me! You know when I sit down and when I rise up; you discern my thoughts from afar. You search out my path and my lying down and are acquainted with all my ways. Even before a word is on my tongue, behold, O Lord, you know it altogether." (Psalm 139 :1–4)

He is preparing a place for me.

"In my Father's house are many mansions; if it were not so, I would have told you; for I go to prepare a place for you. And if I go and prepare a place for you, I come again, and will receive you unto myself; that where I am, there ye may be also." (John 14:2–3)

He is exceeding my expectations.

As fabulous as I can envision a mansion in heaven, this one will be better. "As it is written, 'What no eye has seen, nor ear heard, nor the heart of man imagined, what God has prepared for those who love him.'" (1 Corinthians 2:9)

I have lost the desire for a stone house. I no longer dream about owning a granite structure in this lifetime, because my Dad is making me one and I can't wait to see it. I still like stone structures and they catch my eye when I drive past them, but the strong desire is gone, replaced with the anticipation of seeing the one He is making for me.

Sharing in His Sufferings

I was driving east on Oregon Road in Lancaster County, Pennsylvania, and had just passed Friendship Community. I was pondering on what it means to share in His sufferings and why we suffered. This phrase is mentioned a few times in the New Testament and it has puzzled me.

"For as we share abundantly in Christ's sufferings, so through Christ we share abundantly in comfort too." (2 Corinthians 1:5)

"That I may know him and the power of his resurrection, and may share his sufferings." (Philippians 3:10)

I decided to ask the Holy Spirit about this concept. He conveyed to my mind it is so we will know more about Jesus. As we hurt, we are walking in His shoes, and we are able to taste how He feels when He suffers.

For example, Jesus loved the world but not every one has returned His love. His care has not been reciprocated. I thought of people who I love and pray for who do not love me back, and I am tempted to remove them from my my mind because I am hurt. Yet, Jesus never does. He continues to love regardless of how people respond for He is love.

Then I thought of how I had borne burdens for people and never been acknowledged or thanked for my effort. But Jesus is continually bearing burdens whether He is thanked or not. As I share in His sufferings in a small way I am developing a deeper understanding of Him and what He must feel.

My Friend the Spirit

I was reading wonderful email testimonials from men who had read my book, The Christian Home and Family Worship. I was wishing there was some friend or family member with whom I could share my excitement.

Then I was reminded of my friend the Spirit who is with me forever. I also recalled the scripture where Jesus rejoiced in the Spirit. It was a lovely time of communion. That day I rejoiced in and with the Holy Spirit. He is a friend who sticks closer than a brother.

"I will ask the Father, and He will give you another Helper, to be with you forever." (John 14:16)

"In that same hour He rejoiced in the Holy Spirit." (Luke 10:21)

"A man of many companions may come to ruin, but there is a friend who sticks closer than a brother." (Proverbs 18:24)

His Father Saw Him and Felt Compassion

John was sleeping in the passenger seat as we were driving on the Pennsylvania Turnpike towards New Wilmington, Pennsylvania to meet my friends Andy and Dr. MacKenzie. I was listening to the song called "Abba Father" by Steve Fry. I had a picture in my mind of an overview of my life in which I was always busy doing things, with lots of friends and activities. In the background, silent and very large, was God, always present and patiently seeking to draw me in to His bosom.

I saw Him as a large loving Dad, a huge being, surrounded by the clouds, watching and yearning to have a heart relationship with me. He has observed all of my hurts, known all I have done, watched the people I have been with, and He was always present, but in the background. This knowledge that He has always been with me, and in His gentle way patiently drew me to Himself, brought tears to my eyes. I still weep at the concept and the reality of the love and care of my Father.

I have always missed having an intimate relationship with my Dad as a child, which I'm sure contributes to how much I still long to be seen, known, and embraced by my Abba, Father.

"The God who made the world and everything in it, being Lord of heaven and earth, does not live in temples made by man, He is actually not far from each one of us, for 'In him we live and move and have our being.'" (Acts 17:24, 27-28)

"One God and Father of all, who is over all and through all and in all." (Ephesians 4:6)

"He arose and came to his father. But while he was still a long way off, his father saw him and felt compassion, and ran and embraced him and kissed him." (Luke 15:20)

He Sees Me

For our 35th anniversary, Sandi and I made a special trip to Mackinac Island, Michigan for the annual Lilac Festival. The first few days we rode bikes, took a tour of the island, hiked to the fort to see the sunset, and took in the primary attractions. After we had a good sense of what the island had to offer, we then spent a day or two pursuing our own separate interests.

Because I like history I headed for the stone walls of Fort Mackinac to learn from the costumed interpreters. Just outside of the gate stands Trinity Church, an old Episcopal Church which was built in 1837. A carpenter was at work on the front door and gave me permission to see the inside of the church. I found my way to a simple wood pew and reverently sat down, soaking in the stillness. On the wall at the front of the sanctuary were these words, "The Lord is in his holy temple." The inspiration for this verse could have originated from either of these passages.

"The Lord is in his holy temple; the Lord's throne is in heaven; his eyes see." (Psalms 11:4)

"The Lord is in his holy temple; let all the earth keep silence before him." (Habakkuk 2:20)

As I sat there in the presence of God, I was keenly aware that God sees me. The God of eternity, the everlasting God, sees me, sitting in a simple wood pew in Michigan. I am learning to not quickly turn my attention to something else but let God's truth infuse my heart and mind. He sees me.

I thought of Hagar who had been cast out by Sarah and found herself alone in the wilderness, where the Angel of the Lord found her and spoke with her. Her response was to address God as El Roi, the God who sees or the God of seeing.

"So she called the name of the Lord who spoke to her, 'You are a God of seeing,' for she said, 'Truly here I have seen Him who looks after me.'" (Genesis 16:13)

Prayer

"I remember the days of old; I meditate on all that you have done; I ponder the work of your hands. I stretch out my hands to you; my soul thirsts for you like a parched land.

Let me hear in the morning of your steadfast love, for in you I trust. Make me know the way I should go, for to you I lift up my soul.

Teach me to do your will, for you are my God! Let your good Spirit lead me on level ground!" (Psalms 143:5-6, 8, 10)

QUESTIONS FOR REFLECTION

1. "I didn't simply learn about God, I was enabled to know the living God myself." What does this statement mean to you? Can you explain the differences between learning about God, and learning to know God? Can you identify some ways you have learned ABOUT God, and some ways or times you have actually grown in KNOWING GOD Himself?

2. Knowing God is a "very present help in trouble,"(Psalm 46:1) have you received any divine illuminations during a challenging time in your life?

3. Exchange stories with a friend or study partner, that you may be mutually edified and encouraged! We comprehend the love of God "with all the saints" (Ephesians 3:18).

4. Think about one person you've struggled to like in the past. What about them do you NOT like? Do you agree with Steve's statement, "It is our own pain that hinders us from loving and connecting with others"? Prayerfully, consider how this person brings out the pain and brokenness in you. Ask God for healing in that area of your life. Ask Him to reveal His Love for you, and His Love for that person.

5. Consider these divine illuminations: I Miss You Too, A Stone House, Sharing in His Sufferings, My Friend the Spirit, His Father Saw Him and Felt Compassion, and He Sees Me. Which of them strikes a special chord in YOUR spirit? Why does it draw you? What is God's invitation to you regarding knowing Him in a new way?

CHAPTER 6:
ABIDE IN MY LOVE

"As the Father has loved me, so have I loved you. Abide in my love." John 15:9

The last four words of this pivotal verse are "abide in my love." Abide means to live in or make a place of residence. I have had experiences of knowing God loves me, but the tenor of this phrase is not to simply taste the love of God but to live in it. I am to make His love a permanent place of residence. I believe Jesus is calling each of us to "abide in my love."

A little gem of a verse I found during my study is in Jude:21 "Keep yourselves in the love of God." In addition to this exhortation from Jesus to abide in His love, Jude echoes this same call to the believers he was addressing in the Spirit.

Christian author Elisabeth Elliot had a radio broadcast called "Gateway to Joy" which ran for many years. She often began her episodes with this phrase, "You are loved with an everlasting love" and "underneath are the everlasting arms." (Jeremiah 31:3, Deuteronomy 33:27) We need to know we are loved. We need to be told this wonderful message of good news, often. The steadfast love of God for His children never ceases.

Move at Your Own Pace

The next few chapters are filled with meaty scriptures. You may want to read through them at a normal clip as you have been reading, and then go back and read through more slowly, giving yourself a chance to meditate at your pace. There is an abundance of rich truth here, but it can be overwhelming at one sitting. This book is the distillation of decades of study. Please give yourself time and ask God to reveal what He wants you to see. We all are on the same journey but at different places along the trail!

First Thing in the Morning

I have difficulty believing God loves me when I awaken in the morning. There is a period when I am moving from half awake to awake when I struggle in my mind to be assured of this truth. Thankfully, I am not alone in this adventure. I found comfort in two Psalms making me think perhaps David had similar feelings. When God seems distant and I am unsure of His love, I pray these verses:

"Satisfy us in the morning with your steadfast love, that we may rejoice and be glad all our days." (Psalms 90:14)

"Let me hear in the morning of your steadfast love, for in you I trust." (Psalms 143:8)

I normally personalize the words to make them applicable to my condition. Instead of the plural pronouns "us," "we," and "our," in the first verse I change them to "me," "I," and "my."

"Satisfy me in the morning with your steadfast love, that I may rejoice and be glad all my days." (Revised Psalms 90:14)

His Yoke is Easy

There is no secret how to abide in the love of God. In the next verse Jesus simply, and directly, tells us how to abide. We are to obey Him. "If you keep my commandments, you will abide in my love, just as I have kept my Father's commandments and abide in His love." (John 15:10)

I don't do well with the concept of obedience. Normally when I read language like "keep my commandments" it sounds like law, which is a burden. I received some fresh insight into obeying Jesus as I reread one of my favorite passages of scripture which addresses burdens and the character of Jesus. "Come to me, all who labor and are heavy laden, and I will give you rest. Take my yoke upon you, and learn from me, for I am gentle and lowly in heart, and you will find rest for your souls. For my yoke is easy, and my burden is light." (Matthew 11:28-30)

It seems when Jesus speaks of a yoke, it is a body of doctrine or teaching. The teaching of Jesus was different than the teaching of the Pharisees. The Pharisees sought to impose heavy burdens which were hard to carry. "They tie up heavy burdens, hard to bear, and lay them on people's shoulders." (Matthew 23:4) Jesus warned the disciples to beware of the Pharisees and their teaching. "He began to say unto his disciples first of all, 'Beware of the leaven of the Pharisees, which is hypocrisy.'" (Luke 12:1)

He also warned them about their doctrine. "Then they understood that he did not tell them to beware of the leaven of bread, but of the teaching of the Pharisees and Sadducees." (Matthew 16:12)

The teaching of Jesus is different from the Pharisees. It is a yoke which is easy and a light burden. Notice in Matthew 11:29 where Jesus encourages us to "learn of me." He wants us to forsake the teaching of the religious leaders and learn a new doctrine from Him, which is doable. "This is the love of God, that we keep His commandments. And His commandments are not burdensome." (1 John 5:3)

In reality, the teaching of Jesus is really quite simple: love God with everything in us, and love others as we have been loved. But this problem of "adding to" spiritual doctrine is a temptation that began in ancient history with the pharisees, and persists in nagging all religious leaders today. In the early church, Paul battled these harmful "extrea" or "add-on" teachings. May his ringing declaration reverberate today and deliver us from false shepherds who continue to add burdens too heavy to bear. "For freedom Christ has set us free. Stand firm, therefore, and do not submit again to a yoke of slavery." (Galatians 5:1)

Be Still and Know

I continue to invest time reveling in the presence of God and soaking in the truth of God's love. As this truth penetrates deeper into my heart and mind, that God likes me for who I am and not based on what I do, I am being transformed. Transformation and change take time and intentionality. The more

I comprehend the unconditional love of God, the better equipped I am to give this same kind of love thus fulfilling the new commandment. For he says in John 13:34, "A new commandment I give to you, that you love one another: just as I have loved you."

"Rooted" and "grounded" are two meaningful words Paul used in his prayer in Ephesians 3:17-19. "That Christ may dwell in your hearts through faith—that you, being rooted and grounded in love, may have strength to comprehend with all the saints what is the breadth and length and height and depth, and to know the love of Christ that surpasses knowledge."

Rooted and grounded speak to me of soil and planting. In this vein consider the parable of the sower. "A sower went out to sow his seed. And as he sowed, some fell along the path and was trampled underfoot, and the birds of the air devoured it. And some fell on the rock, and as it grew up, it withered away, because it had no moisture. And some fell among thorns, and the thorns grew up with it and choked it. And some fell into good soil and grew and yielded a hundredfold." As he said these things, he called out, "He who has ears to hear, let him hear." (Luke 8:5-8)

And when his disciples asked him what this parable meant, he said, "To you it has been given to know the secrets of the kingdom of God, but for others they are in parables, so that 'seeing they may not see, and hearing they may not understand.' Now the parable is this: The seed is the word of God. The ones along the path are those who have heard; then the devil comes and takes away the word from their hearts, so that they may not believe and be saved. And the ones on the rock are those who, when they hear the word, receive it with joy. But these have no root; they believe for a while, and in time of testing fall away. And as for what fell among the thorns, they are those who hear, but as they go on their way they are choked by the cares and riches and pleasures of life, and their fruit does not mature. As for that in the good soil, they are those who, hearing the word, hold it fast in an honest and good heart, and bear fruit with patience." (Luke 8:8-15)

Notice the two verses which speak to the good soil and bearing fruit. "And some fell into good soil and grew and yielded a hundredfold. As he said these things, he called out, 'He who has ears to hear, let him hear.'" (Luke 8:8) "As for that in the good soil, they are those who, hearing the word, hold it fast in an honest and good heart, and bear fruit with patience." (Luke 8:15)

If you are still reading these words, you obviously are hungry and have "ears to hear." You are one of those who "hear the word" and "hold it fast." Holding the word, is guarding it from being stolen by the devil. As you hold it fast you are demonstrating you are not shallow but have depth to endure testing. Those who hear and hold fast, nurture the seeds so they are not "choked by the cares and riches and pleasures of life." They care about the truth. They guard against losing it, and invest time and energy to cultivate the truth until it bears good fruit. Deepening our roots takes time, regular watering, and patience, then good fruit follows.

It is unfortunate that we in the western world often miss the symbolism in Jesus' teachings because we are not an agrarian society. In our way of thinking, we expect our hard work to yield better results. But working harder in an orchard or vineyard does not guarantee a greater yield at harvest time. According to John, "abiding in Christ" leads to bearing fruit for Christ. "Abide in me, and I in you. As the branch cannot bear fruit by itself, unless it abides in the vine, neither can you, unless you abide in me. I am the vine; you are the branches. Whoever abides in me and I in him, he it is that bears much fruit, for apart from me you can do nothing." (John 15:4–5)

This is a simple concept and yet it conflicts with how Americans think. We falsely think doing is what matters the most. But in truth, being comes before doing. We need to become human beings, instead of human doings. To the degree we are being and abiding, to the same degree we will be doing good and bearing fruit. Resting in the Lord. Being still. Waiting on God. These are foreign concepts to us, and yet they are the biblical model, and therefore, they work.

"They who wait for the Lord shall renew their strength; they shall mount up with wings like eagles; they shall run and not be weary; they shall walk and not faint." (Isaiah 40:31) We sing songs about this verse, watch movies with this theme, and often memorize it, but we are crippled when it comes to applying it. We are tired, stressed, and often bear little fruit, and we sadly continue to try harder instead of opening the door and having a quiet cup of tea with Jesus each morning.

We have probably all heard sermons about the sisters, Mary and Martha. "Now as they went on their way, Jesus entered a village. And a woman named Martha welcomed him into her house. And she had a sister called Mary, who sat at the Lord's feet and listened to his teaching. But Martha was distracted with much serving. And she went up to him and said, "Lord, do you not care that my sister has left me to serve alone? Tell her then to help me." But the Lord answered her, "Martha, Martha, you are anxious and troubled about many things, but one thing is necessary. Mary has chosen the good portion, which will not be taken away from her." (Luke 10:38–42)

I have been Martha for much of my Christian life. I am becoming Mary. I can write from both perspectives. When I was like Martha, I was fond of multi-tasking. I always wanted to be busy, rushing through my devotions and everything else so that I could cram more activity into my allotted 24 hours. I rarely said "no" to requests to serve, and I discovered that taking a quick power nap would give me enough energy to keep moving. I enjoyed cafeteria meals in college and seminary because they afforded me the efficiency of a fifteen minute meal, which of course meant I could get back to my to-do list faster. I added people and concerns to my prayer list but rarely found time to effectively intercede.

As Mary, I'm learning how to go to bed earlier, so I can arise early to wait on God and be still. I am becoming a better listener to God instead of rushing through a litany of prayer requests. I am reading more slowly, digesting what I read, journalling and being open for new insights from God. My schedule is not packed full. I occasionally go for walks, and am trying to make time for personal refreshment and reflection. I desire to be a well-watered peaceful garden. I have not arrived and often find myself slipping back into old patterns of hectic activity, but I have tasted this new life and agree with Jesus, one thing is "necessary" and it is the "good portion." (Luke 10:42) Most of the material in this book is a result of early morning study and reflection.

Abiding in the Word

Another way I seek to be consistently living and abiding in His love is to read passages which speak of the love of God for me. There is a rich feast in these inspired words. Perhaps read one a day and meditate on it. Or read a few at a time aloud with your spouse or family.

"Know therefore that the Lord your God is God, the faithful God who keeps covenant and steadfast love with those who love Him and keep

His commandments, to a thousand generations." (Deuteronomy 7:9)

"How precious to me are your thoughts, O God! How vast is the sum of them! If I would count them, they are more than the sand. I awake, and I am still with you." (Psalms 139:17–18)

"This I call to mind, and therefore I have hope: The steadfast love of the Lord never ceases; his mercies never come to an end; they are new every morning; great is your faithfulness. 'The Lord is my portion,' says my soul, 'therefore I will hope in him.'" (Lamentations 3:21–24)

"He brought me to the banqueting house, and his banner over me was love." (Song of Solomon 2:4)

"I am my beloved's and my beloved is mine." (Song of Solomon 6:3)

"I am my beloved's, and his desire is for me." (Song of Solomon 7:10)

"The Lord appeared to him from far away. I have loved you with an everlasting love; therefore I have continued my faithfulness to you." (Jeremiah 31:3)

"The Lord your God is in your midst, a mighty one who will save; He will rejoice over you with gladness; He will quiet you by his love; He will exult over you with loud singing." (Zephaniah 3:17)

"And he arose and came to his father. But while he was still a long way off, his father saw him and felt compassion, and ran and embraced him and kissed him. And the son said to him, 'Father, I have sinned against heaven and before you. I am no longer worthy to be called your son.' But the father said to his servants, 'Bring quickly the best robe, and put it on him, and put a ring on his hand, and shoes on his feet. And bring the fattened calf and kill it, and let us eat and celebrate. For this my son was dead, and is alive again; he was lost, and is found.' And they began to celebrate." (Luke 15:20–24)

"For God so loved the world, that He gave his only Son, that whoever believes in Him should not perish but have eternal life. For God did not send His Son into the world to condemn the world, but in order that the world might be saved through Him." (John 3:16–17)

"This is my commandment, that you love one another as I have loved you." (John 15:12)

"The Father Himself loves you, because you have loved me and have believed that I came from God." (John 16:27)

"I made known to them your name, and I will continue to make it known, that the love with which you have loved me may be in them, and I in them." (John 17:26)

"God's love has been poured into our hearts through the Holy Spirit who has been given to us." (Romans 5:5)

"God shows his love for us in that while we were still sinners, Christ died for us." (Romans 5:8)

"For I am convinced that neither death, nor life, nor angels, nor principalities, nor things present, nor things to come, nor powers, nor height, nor depth, nor any other created thing, shall be able to separate us from the love of God, which is in Christ Jesus our Lord." (Romans 8:38-39)

"But God, being rich in mercy, because of the great love with which he loved us, even when we were dead in our trespasses, made us alive together with Christ— by grace you have been saved and raised us up with him and seated us with him in the heavenly places in Christ Jesus, so that in the coming ages he might show the immeasurable riches of his grace in kindness toward us in Christ Jesus. For by grace you have been saved through faith. And this is not your own doing; it is the gift of God, not a result of works, so that no one may boast. For we are his workmanship, created in Christ Jesus for good works, which God prepared beforehand, that we should walk in them."
(Ephesians 2:4-10)

"Christ also loved you, and gave Himself up for us," (Ephesians 5:2)

"But when the goodness and loving kindness of God our Savior appeared, he saved us, not because of works done by us in righteousness, but according to his own mercy, by the washing of regeneration and renewal of the Holy Spirit, whom he poured out on us richly through Jesus Christ our Savior, so that being justified by his grace we might become heirs according to the hope of eternal life." (Titus 3:4-7)

"See what kind of love the Father has given to us, that we should be called children of God; and so we are." (1 John 3:1)

"By this we know love, that He laid down His life for us." (1 John 3:16)

"This is love, not that we have loved God but that He loved us and sent his Son to be the propitiation for our sins." (1 John 4:10)

"So we have come to know and to believe the love that God has for us. God is love, and whoever abides in love abides in God, and God abides in him." (1 John 4:16)

"We love because He first loved us." (1 John 4:19)

Prayer
"Keep yourselves in the love of God." (Jude 21)

QUESTIONS FOR REFLECTION

1. What does this statement mean to you: "I am to make His love a permanent place of residence"? Or as Jude phrases it, "Keep yourself in the love of God."

2. "It is the nature of religious leaders, not only Pharisees, to add to the simple doctrine of Jesus which is to love God with everything in us, and to love others as we have been loved." Which scriptures can you meditate on in order to combat those ideas?

3. Compare the phrase "You cannot give what you do not possess" with what Steve proposes, "The more I comprehend the unconditional love of God, the better equipped I am to give this same kind of love and fulfill the new commandment… 'that you love one another: just as I have loved you'" (John 13:34). Can you think of ways this truth is evidenced in your life?

4. If you are hungry to move more towards becoming a "human being" rather than a "human doing," how could you order your day to spend some time, even a few minutes, to rest in the Lord, be still, and abide in His love?

5. Choose a few verses in this chapter on which to meditate, read aloud, or memorize on, to help these truths sink in. Try to can personalize them by putting your name or "I, me, my" in the verses, as you speak them aloud while your Heavenly Dad listens. Remember He LIKES you!

CHAPTER 7: KNOW THE TRUTH TO BE SET FREE

There are two concepts that govern this section, transformation and truth. If I am going to act properly I need to think properly. "As he thinketh in his heart, so is he." (Proverbs 23:7 KJV) We each have default patterns of thinking which govern our behavior. While Jesus dwells in my heart through faith and graciously gives me a new heart, my mind also needs to be changed. This process is described in the passage, "Do not be conformed to this world, but be transformed by the renewal of your mind." (Romans 12:2)

"Jesus said to the Jews who had believed him, 'If you abide in my word, you are truly my disciples, and you will know the truth, and the truth will set you free.'" (John 8:31-32) When I couple the thought of "to be transformed by the renewal of the mind" with "knowing the truth" I conclude for life-changing transformation to occur, I need to immerse myself in the truth of God's inspired word.

The best way I know to illustrate this idea is through a personal testimony which is hard to put in print since it involves my dear mother. But since this concept is so important I will share it with you.

Since the summer of 2014, God has made me know when I should get up and meet with Him. I was pretty faithful for quite a season, but one morning

I was really tired, and after looking at the clock, rolled over and went back to sleep for another hour.

When I did get up and was heading for the living room to read my Bible I sensed God had a look of disappointment on His face. I had seen this look before on the face of my Mom and it was not an encouraging one. I was feeling sad and a little condemned because I felt I had let God down, when He gently whispered, "I'm not your Mom. I love you all the time."

Please understand I do not want to disrespect or belittle my mother, nor am I implying she did not love me well. But I want to let you in on the internal "conversation" I had with God that morning which overturned a stronghold in my mind . Even though I knew my Mom loved me, I often felt I could not please her and at those times saw a look of disappointment on her face.

God was reminding me He is not only loving, He is love, and He never changes. He loves me regardless of when I arise in the morning. His commands and instructions are given for my good. He does not suffer when I do not do what I am called to do, I am the one who missed out on an hour of fellowship with my Dad.

Parents are human. They give it their best shot, but often miss the mark. God never does. I have spent time reflecting on how I view God as I seek to see Him and His character through the lens of scripture and not how I viewed my own Dad.

My Dad was a faithful provider, and honorable man, a kind husband, but we did not connect emotionally. He was a nice man, loved by all who knew him, a born salesman, and always available when I needed him. I loved and admired him. He was my Dad. But relationally he was distant, it was not easy for me to talk to him, and I didn't feel he understood me. Our common ground in later years was playing golf. We played once or twice a year and I thoroughly enjoyed being with him on the course.

I have found myself seeing God in a similar fashion. A really nice guy, everyone appreciates Him, He is present in emergencies, kind, honorable, but doesn't know me, nor connect emotionally with me. I know now, these impressions are not biblical but they are a part of who I am, and I have to purposefully replace them with correct thinking.

I am aware that believing God loves me at all times is one of my weak spots, so I am intentional about reading passages about God's grace, His affection, His unchangeable character, and how He is always for me. The more I am exposed to these powerful truths, I am set free from old patterns of thinking and transformed in my mind.

In this first illustration, the problem is my own head and my past experiences which continue to influence me. The battle for me is to let go of old ways of looking at truth and to embrace the new insights He has been revealing to me. I readily acknowledge I have patterns of thinking which are not accurate. I think of these as my default settings.

Whenever I purchase a new phone or computer, I have to go into the settings and change fonts and other preprogrammed information.

Putting off the old man takes time and energy. "Put off your old self, which belongs to your former manner of life and is corrupt through deceitful desires." (Ephesians 4:22) While Paul encourages us to put off, he also exhorts us to put on. "Be renewed in the spirit of your minds, and to put on the new self, created after the likeness of God in true righteousness and holiness." (Ephesians 4:23–24)

Many well meaning authors have written devotionals to encourage people, but while these are pleasant reading, the word of God makes the most impact in transforming my mind.

"All Scripture is breathed out by God and profitable for teaching, for reproof, for correction, and for training in righteousness" (2 Timothy 3:16).

"The word of God is living and active, sharper than any two-edged sword, piercing to the division of soul and of spirit, of joints and of marrow, and discerning the thoughts and intentions of the heart." (Hebrews 4:12)

"Heaven and earth will pass away, but my words will not pass away." (Matthew 24:35)

New Every Morning

Over the past few years I have put together many "meditations" and "affirmations" which I read regularly. These topical studies help me overcome and confront lies and untruths. The most recent one I have completed is a series of scriptures which testify "Who I Am in Christ." These lists help me believe the truth while transforming and rebuilding my thinking. You can find more at www. buildingfaithfamilies.org/knowinggodslove/

"The faithful love of the LORD never ends! His mercies never cease. Great is his faithfulness; his mercies begin afresh each morning." (Lamentations 3:22–23 NLT)

As mentioned previously, another battle I confront most mornings, is feeling God is physically and emotionally distant from me. In response to this need, I have assembled scriptures which assure me when I draw near to Him, He always draws near to me in love. Here are some of my favorite verses to combat this untruth.

"Draw near to God, and He will draw near to you." (James 4:8)

"In Him we live and move and have our being." (Acts 17:28)

"Satisfy us in the morning with your steadfast love, that we may rejoice and be glad all our days." (Psalms 90:14)

"Let me hear in the morning of your steadfast love, for in you I trust." (Psalms 143:8)

Fear

Since 2012 I have been helped to identify an unrecognized fear, which has played a part in shaping my life. Through the help of trained counselors and the good Spirit, I have faced the source of my angst; which is the fear of being abandoned. You may already know which scriptures I cling to when I am tempted to feel alone and forsaken.

"Behold, I am with you always, to the end of the age." (Matthew 28:20)

"I will ask the Father, and He will give you another Helper, to be with you forever." (John 14:16)

"I will never leave you nor forsake you." (Hebrews 13:5)

"There is no fear in love, but perfect love casts out fear. For fear has to do with punishment, and whoever fears has not been perfected in love. (1 John 4:18)

Daily Studies

We each need to work out our own salvation with fear and trembling, but what I do most days is read a page of scriptures to prepare my heart to meet God. I have six of these, one for each day of the week. They are similar to a call to worship. There are seventeen subsections where I read the passage(s) and then pause to apply it. For example the first one is Draw Near to God. I read the verses and then consciously look to God and focus on Him.

Here is the first set to give you a taste. If these are a help to you, you may access the other five at www. BuildingFaithFamilies.org and select the Building a Family of Faith Series, or go directly to this address, www.buildingfaithfamilies.org/knowinggodslove/. Meditation 1 of 6 which I read in the morning.

Draw near

"It is good to be near God; I have made the Lord GOD my refuge," (Psalms 73:28)

"Seek the LORD while he may be found; call upon him while he is near;" (Isaiah 55:6)

Be thankful

"Enter his gates with thanksgiving, and his courts with praise! Give thanks to him; bless his name!" (Psalms 100:4)

God's love

"This I know, that God is for me." (Psalms 56:9)

"This is love, not that we have loved God but that he loved us and sent his Son to be the propitiation for our sins." (1 John 4:10)

Present yourself

"Present yourselves to God as those who have been brought from death to life, and your members to God as instruments for righteousness. (Romans 6:13)

Cleansing

"Wash me thoroughly from my iniquity, and cleanse me from my sin! For I know my transgressions, and my sin is ever before me." (Psalms 51:2-3)

Prepare your heart

"Let your heart therefore be wholly true to the LORD our God, walking in his statutes and keeping his commandments, as at this day." (1 Kings 8:61)

Spirit of God

"Be filled with the Spirit." (Ephesians 5:18)

Word of God

"The word of God is living and active, sharper than any two-edged sword, piercing to the division of soul and of spirit, of joints and of marrow, and discerning the thoughts and intentions of the heart." (Hebrews 4:12)

Transformed in truth

"Jesus said to the Jews who had believed him, 'If you abide in my word, you are truly my disciples, and you will know the truth, and the truth will set you free.'" (John 8:31-32)

Worship God

"Worthy are you, our Lord and God, to receive glory and honor and power, for you created all things, and by your will they existed and were created." (Revelation 4:11)

Submit your will

"Submit yourselves therefore to God." (James 4:7)

Commit

"Trust in the LORD with all your heart, and do not lean on your own understanding. In all your ways acknowledge him, and he will make straight your paths." (Proverbs 3:5-6)

Abide

"God is love, and whoever abides in love abides in God, and God abides in him." (1 John 4:16)

Sovereign Lord

"Yours, O LORD, is the greatness and the power and the glory and the victory and the majesty, for all that is in the heavens and in the earth is yours. Yours is the kingdom, O LORD, and you are exalted as head above all. Both riches and honor come from you, and you rule over all. In your hand are power and might, and in your hand it is to make great and to give strength to all. And now we thank you, our God, and praise your glorious name." (1 Chronicles 29:11–13)

Trust

"Those who know your name put their trust in you, for you, O LORD, have not forsaken those who seek you." (Psalms 9:10)

Joy

"Let all who take refuge in you rejoice; let them ever sing for joy, and spread your protection over them, that those who love your name may exult in you. For you bless the righteous, O LORD; you cover him with favor as with a shield." (Psalms 5:11–12)

Wait

"The Lord is good to those who wait for him, to the soul who seeks him. It is good that one should wait quietly for the salvation of the Lord." (Lamentations 3:25–26)

Jesus

"Christ Jesus, who, though he was in the form of God, did not count equality with God a thing to be grasped, but made himself nothing, taking the form of a servant, being born in the likeness of men. And being found in human form, he humbled himself by becoming obedient to the point of death, even death on a cross." (Philippians 2:5–8)

Strength for today and bright hope for tomorrow

May "the LORD bless you and keep you; the LORD make his face to shine upon you and be gracious to you; the LORD lift up his countenance upon you and give you peace." (Numbers 6:24–26)

After I work through the meditation, I then read the chapters assigned for my daily Bible reading which I have been following for over thirty years. I know myself and without a schedule I will not be able to read through the Bible each year. I don't think everyone needs to do this, but it is the best habit I have ever made. The schedule I follow has a New Testament or Psalms portion along with an Old Testament section. These schedules can be found at www.BuildingFaithFamilies.org and select Bible Resources. On this page, in blue rectangles, are the schedules.

Depending on my own needs each day, I might also read a study that focuses on some aspect of truth that will encourage me. Here is a portion of one I pulled together about what God has done for each of us. Reading it inspires me to give thanks.

Thank you for ...

Creating me in your image

"So God created man in his own image, in the image of God he created him; male and female he created them." (Genesis 1:27)

Knowing me

"I praise you, for I am fearfully and wonderfully made. Wonderful are your works; my soul knows it very well. My frame was not hidden from you, when I was being made in secret, intricately woven in the depths of the earth." (Psalm 139:14–15)

Choosing me

"He chose us in him before the foundation of the world." (Ephesians 1:4)

Liking me

"How precious to me are your thoughts, O God! How vast is the sum of them!" (Psalm 139:17)

Being on my team

"This I know, that God is for me." (Psalms 56:9)

Having my back

"So we can confidently say, 'The Lord is my helper; I will not fear; what can man do to me?'" (Hebrews 13:6)

Being made sin for me

"For our sake he made him to be sin who knew no sin." (2 Corinthians 5:21)

Taking away my sin

"Behold, the Lamb of God, who takes away the sin of the world." (John 1:29)

Being pierced and crushed for my sin

"He was pierced for our transgressions; he was crushed for our transgressions." (Isaiah 53:5)

Delivering me from condemnation

"There is therefore now no condemnation for those who are in Christ Jesus." (Romans 8:1)

I will be placing more of these studies online for those who are interested at www.buildingfaithfamilies.org/knowinggodslove/. Thankfully, my mind is being transformed, freeing me from my unbiblical default settings and replacing them with eternal truth.

Besides my own head, I also have an enemy whose whole being is devoted to tearing down and destroying what is true. "The thief comes only to steal and kill and destroy. I came that they may have life and have it abundantly." (John 10:10) The more I embrace the truth of God's love, the better equipped I am to love God and my family. It is no wonder the devil is seeking to destroy my relationship with God and an accurate apprehension of grace.

As we set ourselves to hold on to truth, we are confronting strongholds, lies, misinformation, and unscriptural teaching. We are now engaged in a life and death struggle for the truth which Jesus came to give us. He came to set us free from untruth, unbelief, sin, and satan. He also came to give us life abundantly.

Just as Jesus confronted lies with the sword of the Spirit, the eternal word of God, so must we. The truth transforms, it sets me free from untruths, and it is a weapon to counteract the lies from the liar and deceiver.

Prayer

"Though we walk in the flesh, we do not war according to the flesh (for the weapons of our warfare are not of the flesh, but mighty before God to the casting down of strongholds), casting down imaginations, and every high thing that is exalted against the knowledge of God, and bringing every thought into captivity to the obedience of Christ." (1 Corinthians 10:3-5)

Father grant us an appetite for grace and truth, which meet in Jesus. Amen.

QUESTIONS FOR REFLECTION

1. "We each have default patterns of thinking that govern our behavior," Steve suggests in the beginning of this chapter. What is one of your default patterns? Fill in the blanks: When _____ (a person) says/does _____ (these words/an action), I respond by _____ (another action).

2. If you are willing, think about your earthly parents. Respectfully but honestly examine which words or actions of your earthly parents affect how you view your heavenly Dad. How can you go about "letting go of old ways of looking at truth" and "embracing new insights God is revealing to you?

3. Steve shares a story of how God spoke encouraging words to him after he felt that he disappointed God by not getting up early to meet with Him. Describe the words or actions here, and talk to God about them. Ask Him to shed light on how He truly feels about you. Ask your Heavenly Dad to change your "default settings" to reflect His TRUTH.

4. Why is the devil seeking to destroy your relationship with God and your accurate comprehension, or grasp, of grace?

5. Choose one or more of the "call to worship" sets in the chapter and in Appendix B. As you are led, find a way to incorporate them into your day. Maybe you could record the sets of verses on your phone or iPod and listen as you drive. "All scripture is breathed out by God and profitable!" (2 Timothy 3:16)

CHAPTER 8:
FAITH COMES
BY HEARING

As Christians, everything we hold dear requires a measure of faith: the creation and purpose of our world; the forgiveness of sin; the resurrection of Christ; our future home in heaven. Even receiving the biblical truth that God likes, loves and adores us requires faith. Paul succinctly said it in 2 Corinthians 5:7, "We walk by faith, not by sight."

"Faith is the assurance of things hoped for, the conviction of things not seen." (Hebrews 11:1) The operative words here are "assurance" and "conviction," for faith is more than hoping or wishing. Faith is a calm assurance and a rock solid conviction.

One of the heroes of faith, who is referred to as "father of all them that believe," (Romans 4:11) is Abraham. If you aren't familiar with this Godly man, read the story of his life in Genesis 12-25. He is mentioned over 280 times in 27 books of the Bible. I generally try to quote scripture which I reference in a verse or two, but this passage is so rich I could not bear to shorten it.

> "That is why it depends on faith, in order that the promise may rest on grace and be guaranteed to all His offspring— not only to the adherent of the law but

also to the one who shares the faith of Abraham, who is the father of us all, as it is written, 'I have made you the father of many nations'—in the presence of the God in whom he believed, who gives life to the dead and calls into existence the things that do not exist. In hope he believed against hope, that he should become the father of many nations, as he had been told, 'So shall your offspring be.' He did not weaken in faith when he considered his own body, which was as good as dead (since he was about a hundred years old), or when he considered the barrenness of Sarah's womb. <u>No unbelief made him waver concerning the promise of God, but he grew strong in his faith as he gave glory to God, fully convinced that God was able to do what he had promised.</u> That is why his faith was 'counted to him as righteousness.' But the words 'it was counted to him' were not written for his sake alone, but for ours also. It will be counted to us who believe in Him who raised from the dead Jesus our Lord, who was delivered up for our trespasses and raised for our justification." (Romans 4:16–25)

Verse 20 is particularly meaningful as a description of faith in action. Abraham, a centenarian, was physically unable to conceive children since his body "was as good as dead." Even though he lacked the natural ability, he continued to believe what God had said. He was "fully convinced that God was able to do what he had promised." This is faith. Not looking to ourselves, but to God and His promises.

But what if we do not have faith like Abraham? We can ask God to give us faith and help our unbelief as did the father of the child who could not speak. "Jesus said to him, 'If you can'! All things are possible for one who believes. Immediately the father of the child cried out and said, 'I believe; help my unbelief!'" (Mark 9:23-24)

In addition to asking God to help our unbelief I have found reading and hearing the word of God strengthens my belief and stimulates my faith. "Faith comes from hearing, and hearing through the word of Christ." (Romans 10: 17) I have found the more time I spend in the word of God, the better my eternal perspective. If I read only the newspaper I generally get discouraged, but if I read the faith-building word of God, I get encouraged.

Hope also grows when exposed to the inspired text. "For whatever was written in former days was written for our instruction, that through endurance and through the encouragement of the Scriptures we might have hope." (Romans 15:4)

As a Christian, called to walk by faith, spending time daily in the word of God is vital. I have practiced the daily discipline of reading some portion of scripture for over thirty years. This is the single most important habit God has helped me to maintain, and my faith has been immeasurably strengthened as a result.

Work of God

Some might say you either have faith or you don't. I acknowledge some members of the body of Christ have the gift of faith. This is a unique and special calling. But all believers possess some measure of faith. Faith is a muscle we need to exercise to develop. Reading and hearing the inspired word of God is one way. Asking God to help us is another way. Each of us needs to give heed to developing faith. I am like the father in Mark 9:24 "I believe; help my unbelief!" Learning what helps us believe and identifying what hinders us will be unique to each of us. Faith is foundational work. "Jesus answered them, 'This is the work of God, that you believe in Him whom He has sent.'" (John 6:29)

Believing and Knowing

"Knowing" is a word which is similar to "believing," or possessing "faith." In some ways knowing is stronger than hoping. It is a firm and settled knowledge. In the book of 1 John there are 38 references to the word "know" or "knows." John wasn't writing about hoping, aspiring, or wishing, but knowing. John was convinced that our faith could be so certain that we could "know". Here is a sampling from 1 John.

"We know that we have passed out of death into life, because we love the brothers." (1 John 3:14)

"By this we know love, that He laid down his life for us, and we ought to lay down our lives for the brothers." (1 John 3:16)

In my early years as a new creature in Christ, I received a wonderful piece of advice from a mature believer. He encouraged me to memorize 1 John 1:9 which says "If we confess our sins, He is faithful and righteous to forgive us our sins and to cleanse us from all unrighteousness." This brother in Christ counseled me that when I sinned I was to ask God to forgive my sin, and then believe He would, regardless of what I felt. He said it was important to learn this verse because I would be tempted to not believe I was forgiven because I might not feel forgiven. In order to combat doubt, unbelief, and unreliable emotions, I needed to train myself to believe the truth. I am so thankful I learned this principle from the beginning of my faith walk. Over the years I have added other passages to reinforce the eternal fact of the blessed gift of forgiveness. Two Psalms of David are replete with the good news.

"Have mercy on me, O God, according to your steadfast love; according to your abundant mercy blot out my transgressions. Wash me thoroughly from my iniquity, and cleanse me from my sin!" (Psalms 51:1-2)

"Purge me with hyssop, and I shall be clean; wash me, and I shall be whiter than snow. Let me hear joy and gladness; let the bones that you have broken rejoice. Hide your face from my sins, and blot out all my iniquities. Create in me a clean heart, O God, and renew a right spirit within me." Psalms 51:7-10)

"Bless the LORD, O my soul, and all that is within me, bless his holy name! Bless the LORD, O my soul, and forget not all his benefits, who forgives all your iniquity," (Psalms 103:1-3)

"He does not deal with us according to our sins, nor repay us according to our iniquities. For as high as the heavens are above the earth, so great is his steadfast love toward those who fear him; as far as the east is from the west, so far does he remove our transgressions from us." (Psalms 103:10-12)

In the same way, I have a tendency to doubt God loves me. I am tempted to lean on my feelings when God seems distant, or not pleased with me. This is where I need to stand on the facts of God's truth to combat unbelief. The truth is God loves and likes me, just as I am. Just as I have learned to embrace God's forgiveness by faith, I am also learning to accept His affectionate care and love by faith. "This I call to mind, and therefore I have hope: The steadfast love of the Lord never ceases; his mercies never come to an end." (Lamentations 3:21-22)

Here are a few more passages which encourage me to believe.

"Without faith it is impossible to please Him, for whoever would draw near to God must believe that He exists and that He rewards those who seek Him." (Hebrews 11:6)

"By faith Sarah herself received power to conceive, even when she was past the age, since she considered him faithful who had promised." (Hebrews 11:11)

"His divine power has granted to us all things that pertain to life and godliness, through the knowledge of Him who called us to His own glory and excellence, by which He has granted to us His precious and very great promises, so that through them you may become partakers of the divine nature." (2 Peter 1:3–4)

Prayer

We believe, but help our unbelief. Strengthen our faith and teach us how to be fully assured and thoroughly convinced of the inspired truths in your word. For "without faith it is impossible to please Him, for whoever would draw near to God must believe that He exists and that He rewards those who seek Him." (Hebrews 11:6)

QUESTIONS FOR REFLECTION

1. How is faith like a muscle we need to exercise? Explain why it is "important work" to believe.

2. What unique ways has God provided to develop faith in your life?

3. What hinders your faith?

4. Can you identify with Steve when he says that he has a tendency to doubt that God forgives him, and doubt that God loves him?

5. Think about times when you have sinned or done wrong things. Discuss how your feelings get in the way of believing God's promises about forgiveness and love.

CHAPTER 9: COMPREHENDING WITH ALL THE SAINTS

"That you(plural), being rooted and grounded in love, may have strength to comprehend with all the saints what is the breadth and length and height and depth, and to know the love of Christ." (Ephesians 3:17-19) I have a tendency to read the scriptures in the first person. But this passage is taken from a letter the apostle Paul addressed to the church in Ephesus.

I have heard of a new translation of the New Testament which employs the word "y'all" to emphasize the plural of you. We need other members of the body of Christ to more fully comprehend the love of Christ. We certainly depend on the Spirit and the word of God, but we also need each other to assimilate the dimensions of God's care and affection.

I have spoken of the love my son John has for me and I have for him. It is the nearest I have come to experiencing unconditional love and grace. His love for me is not tied to any performance or accomplishment on my part, but stems from the simple truth, I am his Dad and he is my son. The way John loves me has had a tremendous impact on my understanding of the love God has for me as my Father.

The way my parents loved me has also impacted the way I understand God's love for me. I ready acknowledge I was not an easy son to raise. But through thick or thin they faithfully stood by me. They were always there. I made good decisions and bad decisions, and they never strayed from my corner supporting me even when they didn't understand or agree with my choices. I could always count on them. Our parent child bond was strong and constant.

John likes me, but he doesn't always understand or know me as well as my wife knows me. She has much better insight into my character and moods and loves me still. Her love is different than John's because it is more fully informed, and after thirty plus years together we have chosen to continue to love and support each other. We have grown in our appreciation and understanding of each other. After making our way through deep waters in 2011 and 2012, we are now in the best place we have ever been.

Next to my parents and my wife, I have three incredible sons who also know me. They too have seen the good, the bad, and the ugly, and have chosen to forgive me and stand by me. Their love is different than John's because they know me better and have more understanding, and yet still choose to stay in our company, live nearby, and be a regular part of my life. I am crying as I write these words. They are examples of grace and love which "covers a multitude of sins." (1 Peter 4:8) I am a rich man for these relationships alone.

God, in His goodness, has also provided me with a large company of loving friends, each of whom have revealed a new facet of God's love to me. The affection we receive from each other is a foretaste of the great love God has for us. I hope we have each had people in our life whose face lights up in a smile when they greet us. I can think of several people whose countenance made me know they liked me. In addition to my parents, I think of my grandparents, Aunt Gloria, Mr. Murray, Dr. MacKenzie, Andy Toncic, and several others. As Clarence said the movie "It's A Wonderful Life", "No man is a failure who has friends." I am not a failure for I have wonderful friends.

The affection we receive from each other is a foretaste of the great love God has for us. These earthly glimpses help us to grasp the heavenly reality of our Father's love which never changes.

Special Emissaries of Love

While all abortion breaks my heart, it is exceptionally grievous to me when I hear of a mother choosing to abort a child with Downs Syndrome or other disabilities. Not only do these precious infants deserve to live, for they are no less created in the image of God than you and I, but we need them. Every part of the body of Christ is necessary for all of us to be properly built up in love. 1 Peter 4:10 says it likes this: "As each has received a gift, use it to serve one another, as food stewards of God's varied grace.

Each part of the body of Christ is necessary for all of us to be properly built up in love. I have the privilege of attending a Joni and Friends Family Retreat each summer. These camps are comprised of families affected by disability. Many people, myself included, believe these weeks are a glimpse of heaven. Love abounds. I could tell you of so many precious people who may not be able to speak, walk, or feed themselves, but they can love. They wonderfully contribute to the body of Christ.

One smile from Laura or Kyle can brighten a whole room. One hug from Mike is worth driving to camp. Upon our arrival at camp, I only had to listen for a loud eruption of joy to discover where Stephen was holding court in his motorized wheelchair. Stephen is unable to do much verbalizing, but he certainly can make you know when he is thrilled to see you.

When our son John saw his counselor from the previous two summers, he ran across the yard and leapt into his arms. I could give even more examples, but I need to ask the rhetorical question, isn't this the way we should all greet each other?

If we want to comprehend and apprehend with all the saints, then we need all the saints! Often I leave camp wondering, "who is disabled?" and "who is normal?" There are only two commands, love God and love each other. According to this measuring stick, these special people are gifted and wonderfully qualified to teach the rest of us about unconditional love and acceptance.

Litmus Test

Not only are we helped to believe His affection by others loving us, we can also gauge our love for God by how we love our neighbor. The love we give and receive amongst ourselves is a two-way street.

"If anyone says, 'I love God,' and hates his brother, he is a liar; for he who does not love his brother whom he has seen cannot love God whom he has not seen. And this commandment we have from him: whoever loves God must also love his brother." (1 John 4:20-21)

1 John has so much rich truth concerning God's love for us. This short but powerful book also speaks candidly about our love for each other. God's love for us, and our love for our brother, go hand in hand.

Whether we are tasting of the love of God or discerning our love for God by how we love our brothers and sisters in Christ, we are comprehending with all the saints, the exceptional love of Christ.

Prayer

Thank you Father for giving us each other. Thank you for friends, family, and special people, who reveal your heart of affection for each one of your children. Thank you for love which covers a multitude of sins. "And may the Lord make you increase and abound in love for one another and for all, as we do for you"
(1 Thessalonians 3:12)

QUESTIONS FOR REFLECTION

1. Think about your view of some passages in the epistles. Do you read them as to you (singular) or to you (plural)? Choose a passage from an epistle that uses "you" and read it aloud, thinking about it being addressed to your church body. How does it change your perspective and interpretation of the passage?

2. Do you know any "special emissaries of love"? If so, describe them briefly here.

3. How do they express love?

4. Think about how easy or hard it is for you to express love. Do you have a revelation of how much God loves you? Ask Him for that revelation.

5. In light of the great commandment to love God with all our heart, soul, mind and strength, should we make this a matter for regular, even daily prayer?

CHAPTER 10: THE GRACE OF JESUS

Peter exhorts us to, "Grow in the grace and knowledge of our Lord and Savior Jesus Christ." (2 Peter 3:18) As we study the grace of Jesus, I hope we will also increase in our knowledge of the person of Jesus. For it is in Jesus we see grace in the flesh. As John 1:17 says, "grace and truth came through Jesus Christ." Just as God is not loving, He is love, so Jesus is not simply gracious, He is grace. I love the phrase in Psalm 85:10 "steadfast love and faithfulness meet; righteousness and peace kiss each other." They meet and kiss each other in our incomparable Savior. God's steadfast love and mercy are not tied to my behavior but to God's character, which never changes.

As I have written earlier, I had long believed the lie that God would love me more if I did more good things for Him. The fruit of this harmful misconception is that while I was pushing and laboring to do good things, it was at the expense of my relationship with a loving, accepting God. Not only that, but my family was subjected to a tired husband and a fragile father. I have difficulty grasping grace and the people closest to me have paid a price as a result of my incorrect and unbiblical thinking.

I am not going to try and define grace, but let the word of God speak. There are two passages which speak of God's mercy and unconditional love. The first doesn't mention the word grace, but describes it nonetheless.

"For while we were still weak, at the right time Christ died for the ungodly. For one will scarcely die for a righteous person—though perhaps for a good person one would dare even to die—but God shows his love for us in that while we were still sinners, Christ died for us." (Romans 5:6-8) God demonstrates, commends, and shows His grace in sending Jesus to die for us while we were most unlovable. Since God loved me while I was a sinner, there is nothing I can do to make God love me more, and there is nothing I can do to make God love me less.

"God, being rich in mercy, because of the great love with which He loved us, even when we were dead in our trespasses, made us alive together with Christ—by grace you have been saved—and raised us up with Him and seated us with Him in the heavenly places in Christ Jesus, so that in the coming ages He might show the immeasurable riches of His grace in kindness toward us in Christ Jesus." (Ephesians 2:4-7)

We will have the coming ages to assimilate the immeasurable riches of God's grace and kindness in sending Jesus to die for us. This gracious act has nothing to do with us; it is all God. As you read the following verses, I hope you will join me in appreciating and growing in the grace and knowledge of Jesus.

"The child grew, and waxed strong, filled with wisdom: and the grace of God was upon him." (Luke 2:40)

"The law was given through Moses; grace and truth came through Jesus Christ." (John 1:17)

"So also is the free gift. For if by the trespass of the one the many died, much more did the grace of God, and the gift by the grace of the one man, Jesus Christ, abound unto the many." (Romans 5:15)

"For if, by the trespass of the one, death reigned through the one; much more shall they that receive the abundance of grace and of the gift of righteousness reign in life through the one, even Jesus Christ." (Romans 5:17)

"Where sin increased, grace abounded all the more, so that, as sin reigned in death, grace also might reign through righteousness leading to eternal life through Jesus Christ our Lord." (Romans 5:20–21)

"By the grace of God I am what I am: and his grace which was bestowed upon me was not found vain; but I labored more abundantly than they all: yet not I, but the grace of God which was with me." (1 Corinthians 15:10)

"For you know the grace of our Lord Jesus Christ, that, though he was rich, yet for your sakes he became poor, that you through his poverty might become rich." (2 Corinthians 8:9) Or as it says in Psalm 18:35, "You have given me the shield of your salvation, and your right hand supported me, and your gentleness made me great."

"For by grace you have been saved through faith; and that not of yourselves, it is the gift of God; not as a result of works, that no one should boast. For we are His workmanship, created in Christ Jesus for good works, which God prepared beforehand, that we should walk in them." (Ephesians 2:8–10)

"For the grace of God has appeared, bringing salvation for all people, training us to renounce ungodliness and worldly passions, and to live self-controlled, upright, and godly lives in the present age." (Titus 2:11–12)

"When the kindness of God our Savior, and his love toward man, appeared, not by works done in righteousness, which we did ourselves, but according to His mercy He saved us, through the washing of regeneration and renewing of the Holy Spirit, which He poured out upon us richly, through Jesus Christ our Savior; that, being justified by His grace, we might be made heirs according to the hope of eternal life." (Titus 3:4–7 NASB)

"We behold him who hath been made a little lower than the angels, even Jesus, because of the suffering of death crowned with glory and honor, that by the grace of God He should taste of death for every man." (Hebrews 2:9)

"It is good for the heart to be strengthened (established) by grace." (Hebrews 13:9)

"You then, my child, be strengthened by the grace that is in Christ Jesus." (2 Timothy 2:1)

"The grace of the Lord Jesus be with the saints."
(Revelation 22:21)

Consider Lovingkindness

Other passages can be found by searching for
the word "grace" in the New Testament. If you want
to broaden the scope of your study, consider the
word "lovingkindness" which is normally rendered
"steadfast love" in newer translations. In the
King James Version, "mercy" is used in place of
"lovingkindness."

I love the word "lovingkindness" and consider it
the Old Testament equivalent of the New Testament
word "grace." Lovingkindness captures the essence
of God's heart. He is slow to anger, merciful,
gracious, and overflowing in lovingkindness and
truth. Here are a few of my favorite passages using
this word in the NASB version.

"The LORD passed by in front of him
and proclaimed, "The LORD, the LORD God,
compassionate and gracious, slow to anger, and
abounding in lovingkindness and truth; who
keeps lovingkindness for thousands, who forgives
iniquity, transgression and sin; yet He will by no
means leave the guilty unpunished, visiting the
iniquity of fathers on the children and on the
grandchildren to the third and fourth generations"
(Exodus 34:6–7 NASB)

"O give thanks to the LORD, for He is good; For
His lovingkindness is everlasting." (1 Chronicles
16:34 NASB)

"Surely goodness and lovingkindness will follow me all the days of my life, And I will dwell in the house of the LORD forever." (Psalm 23:6 NASB)

"All the paths of the LORD are lovingkindness and truth To those who keep His covenant and His testimonies. " (Psalm 25:10 NASB)

"He loves righteousness and justice: The earth is full of the lovingkindness of the Lord." (Psalm 33:5 NASB)

"Thy lovingkindness, O Lord, extends to the heavens; Thy faithfulness reaches to the skies." (Psalm 36:5 NASB)

"Thy lovingkindness is better than life, My lips will praise Thee. So I will bless Thee as long as I live; I will lift up my hands in Thy name." (Psalm 63:3-4 NASB)

"Righteousness and justice are the foundation of Thy throne; Lovingkindness and truth go before Thee." (Psalm 89:14 NASB)

Prayer

"Oh satisfy us in the morning with thy lovingkindness, That we may sing for joy and be glad all our days." (Psalm 90:14 NASB) and "May grace and peace be multiplied to you in the knowledge of God and of Jesus our Lord." (2 Peter 1:2)

QUESTIONS FOR REFLECTION

1. Imagine you are talking to a young believer in Christ about grace, or writing a children's book about grace. How would you describe grace in your own words?

2. "God's steadfast love and mercy are not tied to my behavior but to God's character, which never changes." How is this statement a game-changer for YOUR day-to-day life, in the place where you live right now?

3. Which verse(s) touched your heart and made you want to reread them?

4. Besides meditating on scripture what else can we do to "grow in the grace and knowledge of our Lord and Savior Jesus Christ" (2 Peter 3:18)?

5. What words in the Old Testament are used to render "grace"? Which one or more of these verses gave you additional insight into the concept of grace?

CHAPTER 11:
GOOD SPIRIT

"The grace of the Lord Jesus Christ and the love of God and the fellowship of the Holy Spirit be with you all." (2 Corinthians 13:14) Throughout my journey I have been appreciating the grace of Jesus in a new way, and how he died for me when I was a sinner. I have also been comprehending the love of God, and how much he likes me for who I am and not what I do. The last phrase in this benediction says "the fellowship of the Holy Spirit be with you all."

The choice of words in this passage is interesting. Fellowship, or communion as it is translated in other versions, implies a personal connection. I have often heard about the power, conviction, or inspiration of the Spirit, but this language suggests the third person of the Trinity is indeed a person with whom I can develop a relationship and enjoy the fellowship of His presence. As I pondered this concept, my mind was drawn to a few scriptures shedding more light on the person of the Spirit, and connected with what I had been learning about grace and love.

Apprehending the Love of God

"God's love has been poured into our hearts through the Holy Spirit who has been given to us." (Romans 5:5) The Holy Spirit has a vital role in understanding the love of God. I knew the Spirit brought conviction and was responsible for bringing me to Jesus, but this verse showed me how He had been at the forefront when I asked God to help me love Him with all my heart, soul, mind, and strength. It was the Holy Spirit who poured the love of God into my heart. I had been asking God to move the knowledge of His love from my head to my heart, and He did, through His Spirit.

With Me

"I will pray the Father, and He shall give you another Comforter, that He may be with you for ever." (John 14:16 ASV) In my sorrow, the Comforter had been at my side. I was never alone for He will never leave me. I know this sounds elementary, and it is, but Jesus is not on earth any longer. Jesus, as a human, was limited by time and flesh, and only the men and women who were alive in 33 A.D. could see Him, learn from Him, follow Him. But Jesus is no longer on earth. At present, the Son of God is sitting at the right hand of the Father interceding for us. When Jesus ascended, He ascended into heaven. But the Helper was sent to be with us now. So for the millions of us living beyond 33 A.D. this is wonderful news! Unbound by time, unlimited by culture, race, location, gender, etc., the Holy Spirit is with us and will never leave us. "Nevertheless, I tell you the truth: it is to your advantage that I go away, for if I do not go away, the Helper will not come to you. But if I go, I will send him to you." (John 16:7)

Good Spirit

These past two years I have been developing a new friendship with the Good Spirit. My favorite appellation for the third person of the Trinity is found in Nehemiah 9:20 "You gave your good Spirit to instruct them." Of all the names for the Spirit, I like Good Spirit, because He is good, kind, solid, and a true friend. He is not bizarre. He is faithful, comforting, near, and misunderstood.

I came to realize that I had many misconceptions of who the Holy Spirit is and how He acts on my behalf, and so I determined to search the scriptures diligently, humbly, so that He could straighten out my thinking. Since Jesus said it was to my advantage when He would go to heaven and send the Spirit, then I wanted to know why. At the same time, I wanted to know the Spirit just as I had been coming to know the grace of Jesus and the love of God. Paul prayed I would experience the "fellowship of the Spirit," and I wanted to find the fulfillment of this benediction in 2 Corinthians 13:14 "The grace of the Lord Jesus Christ and the love of God and the fellowship of the Holy Spirit be with you all."

A Faithful Friend

"A man of many companions may come to ruin, but there is a friend who sticks closer than a brother." (Proverbs 18:24)

The Spirit and I are becoming friends. I am learning to be led by Him and enjoy His presence. One morning I awoke and needed to change my socks. I was a little groggy sitting on the edge of my bed when I rolled up one and tossed it in the direction of the clothes hamper in the corner. It was a good shot and sailed right in without touching the sides. I sensed/heard the Good Spirit say "Nice shot" in kind of a cheerful tone. I cocked my head to one side and said, "You're a morning guy huh?" Then we both smiled. It was a precious time and I basked in the wonder of this moment for some time.

I then remembered God doesn't sleep or slumber, which affirms He is indeed a morning guy, all the time. "He will not let you stumble; the one who watches over you will not slumber. Indeed, He who watches over Israel never slumbers or sleeps." (Psalm 121:3-4 NLT)

The Spirit of God is not an It

He is a person, not an influence like wind, not a power source like electricity, not an energy drink like Red Bull. While the Spirit is one with the Father and the Son, He is nonetheless a distinct personage. Notice the pronouns which are used in the following verse. You don't see "it" but "He" and "Him."

"When the Spirit of truth comes, He will guide you into all the truth, for He will not speak on his own authority, but whatever He hears He will speak, and He will declare to you the things that are to come." (John 16:13)

He Teaches and Brings to your Remembrance

"But the Helper, the Holy Spirit, whom the Father will send in my name, He will teach you all things and bring to your remembrance all that I have said to you." (John 14:26)

While I am ever so grateful for the abundance of godly study tools and resource available to me as I endeavor to know and understand God's written word, I lean heavily on the Spirit of God to to unfold and explain scripture to me. The Good Spirit is an excellent tutor and teacher who knows how to convey truth to my mind and heart.

I know the early writers of the four gospels, Matthew, Mark, Luke, and John counted on the Spirit to help them recall the words of Jesus when they compiled their sacred writing. "For no prophecy was ever produced by the will of man, but men spoke from God as they were carried along by the Holy Spirit." (2 Peter 1:21)

He has Feelings and can be Grieved

"Do not grieve the Holy Spirit of God, by whom you were sealed for the day of redemption." (Ephesians 4:30)

One takeaway for me as I read the above passage in Ephesians is that the Holy Spirit has feelings, and I have the potential to grieve Him. I need to learn more about this concept. I know I have grieved the Spirit when I experience conviction and a loss of peace. But I am a novice when it comes to discerning when and how I have offended the Spirit of God.

One takeaway for me when I read this description of the Spirit is I notice He has feelings, and I have the potential to grieve Him. May God help me to not grieve the Gracious Spirit.

He Loves

"I appeal to you, brothers, by our Lord Jesus Christ and by the love of the Spirit." (Romans 15:30)

This is a beautiful expression, "the love of the Spirit". Not only does the Father love us, and the Son of God, but the Spirit loves us as well. Meditating on this truth expands my understanding and appreciation for the Good Loving Spirit.

He Helps us when we are Weak, Intercedes for us, and has a Mind

"Likewise the Spirit helps us in our weakness. For we do not know what to pray for as we ought, but the Spirit Himself intercedes for us with groanings too deep for words. And he who searches hearts knows what is the mind of the Spirit, because the Spirit intercedes for the saints according to the will of God." (Romans 8:26-27)

Many times, when I do not know how to pray, I ask the Spirit to help me and direct my thoughts and words. He has helped me time after time, for He knows the will of God and how to inspire our faith and words. One of the most fulfilling acts I have experienced is praying with a band of like-minded believers and being aware of the Spirit coming upon one after another in powerful anointed prayer.

He is Directing the Affairs of the Church

"Pay careful attention to yourselves and to all the flock, in which the Holy Spirit has made you overseers, to care for the church of God." (Acts 15:28) "For it has seemed good to the Holy Spirit and to us to lay on you no greater burden than these requirements." (Acts 20:28)

I sought God to give me a vision of the church I was serving as an assistant pastor. I earnestly sought God for several weeks. I was looking for a specific plan of action so I could get on board with His strategy. During one of my times of seeking, I realized God has answered my prayer, but in a different way than I expected. He made me know Jesus was the head of the church, and the Spirit was overseeing the administration of His body here on earth. I did not receive a blueprint, but a calm assurance of the headship of Christ and the management of the Spirit.

He Possesses a Will

"All these are empowered by one and the same Spirit, who apportions to each one individually as He wills." (1 Corinthians 12:11)

This lone verse is taken from a longer passage concerning spiritual gifts. What is often lost in listing out the varieties of spiritual gifts and manifestations is the awareness the Holy Spirit is the One who is managing, distributing, and apportioning these divine gifts. He knows the specific needs of each assembly of believers as well as the created personalities and strengths of each person in the family, and He grants spiritual gifts according to His will.

He is God

"Peter said, 'Ananias, why has Satan filled your heart to lie to the Holy Spirit ... You have not lied to man but to God.'" (Acts 5:3-4)

Sometimes I do not know which member of the Trinity to address when praying. In my new relationship with the Spirit, I sometimes say, "Should I be asking you or the Father?" Then I recall the Spirit is God and and thus my question is a moot one.

Jesus and the Holy Spirit

I do not believe Jesus could have fulfilled His earthly mission without the presence and power of the Spirit of God. Beginning with the conception of Jesus in the flesh (see Matt 1:18), followed by His baptism (Matt 3:16) and temptation (Luke 4), and throughout His teaching and healing ministry, we cannot separate the presence and power of the Holy Spirit from the anointed ministry of Jesus.

Jesus Christ. This title is used so often (141 times in the New Testament) we sometimes forget it means Jesus, the Anointed. Christ is not the surname of Jesus. He was anointed by the Holy Spirit. His earthly ministry was a fulfillment and direct result of the prophecy in Isaiah 61:1. Luke references this verse when he writes, "The Spirit of the Lord is upon me, because He has anointed me to proclaim good news to the poor. He has sent me to proclaim liberty to the captives and recovering of sight to the blind, to set at liberty those who are oppressed." (Luke in 4:18)

Jesus depended on the Spirit of God

"Now the birth of Jesus Christ took place in this way. When his mother Mary had been betrothed to Joseph, before they came together she was found to be with child from the Holy Spirit." Matthew 1:18.

"When Jesus was baptized, immediately he went up from the water, and behold, the heavens were opened to him, and He saw the Spirit of God descending like a dove and coming to rest on Him." Matthew 3:16.

"Jesus, full of the Holy Spirit, returned from the Jordan and was led by the Spirit in the wilderness." (Luke 4:1)

"Jesus returned in the power of the Spirit to Galilee, and a report about Him went out through all the surrounding country." (Luke 4:14)

"God anointed Jesus of Nazareth with the Holy Spirit and with power. He went about doing good and healing all who were oppressed by the devil, for God was with Him." (Acts 10:38)

"Behold, my servant whom I have chosen, my beloved with whom my soul is well pleased. I will put my Spirit upon Him, and He will proclaim justice to the Gentiles." (Matthew 12:18)

"If it is by the Spirit of God that I cast out demons, then the kingdom of God has come upon you." (Matthew 12:28)

I think it is significant how powerfully Jesus defends the Holy Spirit when they accused Him of having an unclean spirit. I believe He bristled when He spoke these words of warning."Therefore I tell you, every sin and blasphemy will be forgiven people, but the blasphemy against the Spirit will not be forgiven. And whoever speaks a word against the Son of Man will be forgiven, but whoever speaks against the Holy Spirit will not be forgiven, either in this age or in the age to come." (Matthew 12:31) The unspoken, but clearly communicated message I hear Jesus saying is, "You can say what you want about me, but if you mess with the Holy Spirit I will take you out!"

Through the Eternal Spirit

One of the hidden gems in scripture is the role of the Spirit in the death of Jesus. We know Jesus wrestled in the garden of Gethsemane about drinking the cup of sacrifice. He knew what had to be done, but shrank from it. This conflict within the breast of Jesus was to determine the fate of the human race. If Jesus had weakened in His resolve to die for our sins, billions of people, indeed the whole creation, would have been left without hope. Our future rested in this titanic struggle.

"And they went to a place called Gethsemane. And He said to His disciples, 'Sit here while I pray.'

And He took with Him Peter and James and John, and began to be greatly distressed and troubled. And He said to them, 'My soul is very sorrowful, even to death. Remain here and watch.' And going a little farther, he fell on the ground and prayed that, if it were possible, the hour might pass from him. And he said, 'Abba, Father, all things are possible for you. Remove this cup from me. Yet not what I will, but what you will.'" (Mark 14:32–36)

What made the difference between asking to have the cup pass and then submitting to God's will? I believe a better question is, who made the difference? The answer is found in Hebrews 9:14. "Christ, who through the eternal Spirit offered Himself without blemish to God." The eternal Spirit helped Him to say "nevertheless, not my will, but thine be done."

Jesus was born of the Spirit, filled with the Spirit, led by the Spirit, operated in the power of the Spirit, healed by the Spirit, was anointed by the Spirit, cast out demons by the Spirit, and rejoiced in the Spirit. It was the presence and power of the Spirit which enabled Him to die, and thus fulfill His ministry. If Jesus depended on the Spirit to do what God gave Him to do, then brothers and sisters, so should we.

Pointing to Jesus

This year I am asking the Spirit of truth to reveal Jesus to me as I read through the Old Testament. This is the specialty of the Spirit, for just as Jesus loved and championed the Spirit, the Spirit also loves Jesus and directs our attention to Him.

"When the Helper comes, whom I will send to you from the Father, the Spirit of truth, who proceeds from the Father, He will bear witness about me." (John 15:26)

"He will glorify me, for he will take what is mine and declare it to you." (John 16:14)

I have been asking the Spirit to reveal Jesus in the Old Testament. Whether as the Passover lamb, or as the bread from heaven, the Helper is bearing witness of the person of Jesus throughout scripture.

Ask, Seek, Knock

After Jesus had taught His disciples the Lord's Prayer in Luke 11, He then encouraged them to ask, seek, and knock to receive the Spirit. I am not going to begin a discussion on whether we have to receive the Spirit or whether all believers already possess the Spirit at salvation, I am simply noting the significance of Jesus' words.

"I tell you, ask, and it will be given to you; seek, and you will find; knock, and it will be opened to you. For everyone who asks receives, and the one who seeks finds, and to the one who knocks it will be opened. What father among you, if his son asks for a fish, will instead of a fish give him a serpent; or if he asks for an egg, will give him a scorpion? If you then, who are evil, know how to give good gifts to your children, how much more will the heavenly

Father give the Holy Spirit to those who ask Him!" (Luke 11:9-13)

The Paraclete

Jesus had spent years as a youth and young man becoming acquainted with the Spirit, and then collaborating in harmony with the Spirit during His earthly ministry. He knew the best thing He could do when He ascended was to teach His disciples about the Spirit and encourage them to wait for the coming of the Faithful Comforter, Helper, and Paraclete.

"I tell you the truth: it is to your advantage that I go away, for if I do not go away, the Helper will not come to you. But if I go, I will send Him to you. And when He comes, He will convict the world concerning sin and righteousness and judgment: concerning sin, because they do not believe in me; concerning righteousness, because I go to the Father, and you will see me no longer; concerning judgment, because the ruler of this world is judged." (John 16:7-11)

"When the Spirit of truth comes, He will guide you into all the truth, for He will not speak on his own authority, but whatever He hears he will speak, and He will declare to you the things that are to come. He will glorify me, for He will take what is mine and declare it to you. All that the Father has is mine; therefore I said that He will take what is mine and declare it to you." (John 16:13-15)

Many times I have been reminded of the Spirit's ability to lead me into "all truth". Whether I am teaching math, or looking for an effective way to communicate with a student, the Spirit is on hand to aid me. God is not only Lord of scripture, but Lord of all truth.

Wait

"Behold, I am sending the promise of my Father upon you. But stay in the city until you are clothed with power from on high." (Luke 24:49)

"While staying with them He ordered them not to depart from Jerusalem, but to wait for the promise of the Father, which, He said, 'you heard from me; for John baptized with water, but you will be baptized with the Holy Spirit not many days from now.'" (Acts 1:4–5)

"You will receive power when the Holy Spirit has come upon you, and you will be my witnesses in Jerusalem and in all Judea and Samaria, and to the end of the earth." (Acts 1:8)

Being still, tarrying, and waiting on God are new skills I am developing. Seeking to be clothed, baptized, and empowered is the first step in being an effective witness for God. Doing comes naturally to me. I am learning to tarry and be quiet in the presence of God and His Spirit. These times of connection are becoming the high points in my life.

Be Filled

As Paul enjoined followers of Christ in Ephesians 5:18 to "be filled with the Spirit," may God fill us and reveal more of the person of the Spirit to each thirsty soul.

The primary reason I have included this chapter in the book on the love of the Father is because getting to know the Spirit and having Him "shed abroad the love of God in my heart" (Romans 5:5) has been essential to my knowing God and the love of God. I commend Him to you. He is a wonderful friend who is always near. God the Father is in heaven, Jesus the Son is at His right hand praying for us, but the Comforter has been sent to be with us forever. The church today has full access to the same Spirit as Jesus, Peter, and Paul. "For he gives the Spirit without measure." (John 3:34)

Prayer

"I will ask the Father, and he will give you another Helper, to be with you forever, even the Spirit of truth, whom the world cannot receive, because it neither sees him nor knows him. You know him, for he dwells with you and will be in you." (John 14:16–17) Thank you Jesus, for sending the Spirit to be with us forever.

QUESTIONS FOR REFLECTION

1. What is the Holy Spirit's role according to Romans 5:5? Consider looking it up in other translations to receive a fuller sense of the meaning.

2. What is Steve's favorite appellation for the third person of the Trinity? Copy the verse where he got this from in your own handwriting. Think about it as you write.

3. Steve speaks of the Holy Spirit is as a Person, not a Thing. Which attributes of the person of the Spirit stood out to you? You may want to create a chart with two columns, one entitled "What the Holy Spirit is NOT" and the other "What the Holy Spirit IS."

4. Think about the relationship between Jesus Christ and the Holy Spirit, especially while Jesus lived on earth. Summarize their relationship, using a list of bullet points to record each observation you make.

5. Describe your relationship or how you have experienced "the fellowship of the Holy Spirit" as recorded in the last phrase of 2 Corinthians.

CHAPTER 12:
LET GOD LOVE YOU

As I reflect and recount the blessings of the people I have known and loved, I feel guilty even mentioning my own emotional baggage and issues. I have so much going for me and yet the fact is I do struggle believing I am worthy of the affection of others and especially God Himself. Thankfully my relationship with God has improved dramatically in the past few years. The change did not occur on His side of the equation but on mine.

God's love and affection for me hasn't changed, He is God. He has not become more loving, for He is love. He can't love me more than He already does. The changes have occurred in my own heart. I'm learning to believe God likes me and I am letting God love me. This is an expression which is foreign to many of us. If anyone has a better way of phrasing our part in our relationship with God, I would love to hear it.

"So the LORD must wait for you to come to him so he can show you his love and compassion. For the LORD is a faithful God. Blessed are those who wait for his help." (Isaiah 30:18)

Standing at the Door

I first noticed this concept in scripture when considering the Laodicean Church in the book of Revelation. God is standing at a door knocking.

"Behold, I stand at the door and knock. If anyone hears my voice and opens the door, I will come in to him and eat with him, and he with me." (Revelation 3:20) He is doing His part in reaching out to us, but is behind a closed door. It is our responsibility to open the door and invite Him in.

This passage has often been incorrectly applied to God seeking the lost and the unsaved. These are words for believers in the church, not for unbelievers. God is seeking to be nearer to His own people. They are still following Him, but at a distance. Our Dad desires to be close to us. He wants to share our life with us. We each have the opportunity and the responsibility to open the door and let Him in.

I like to think of God's affection for us like a radio signal or satellite transmission. The signal from heaven is strong and consistent, "God so loves the world" but the static of the world, our own baggage, and the evil one, are all conspiring to inhibit our ability to receive this wonderful truth. It is our job to dial in and access the eternal message of love and acceptance from our Dad.

If God is knocking and you hear His voice whispering to your heart, then open the door and invite Him in.

Like a Hen

Are we willing to let God gather us into His arms? In this passage, Jesus is overlooking Jerusalem, perhaps walking down the road from the Mount of Olives, when he stops and sighs, "O Jerusalem,

Jerusalem, the city that kills the prophets and stones those who are sent to it! How often would I have gathered your children together as a hen gathers her brood under her wings, and you were not willing!" (Luke 13:34)

When we are willing, He is willing to gather us in His arms. The ball is in our court. He is like the father of the prodigal son, standing at the window looking down the street, longing for a glimpse of his son. He is patiently and persistently knocking and whispering to our hearts, always willing to gather us to Himself. But we must turn to Him, open the door and invite Him in.

Crawl Up Into God's Lap

When my son John, who has Down Syndrome, awakes in the morning, he comes downstairs and finds me. If I am standing he hugs me, if I am sitting he crawls into my lap. His hugs are more like holds, for he clings to me for an extended time. But whether standing or sitting, he finds his Dad and we hold each other at the beginning of each day. In this simple act we are communicating our affection for each other. We have been doing this for many years and it is a wonderful way to affirm our continued care for one another.

In the same way, I need to look for God each morning and let Him hold me and love me and make me know I am His kid. God certainly is our Dad and His love does not change, but I am learning

I have to take some initiative to get close to Him. Relationships are always a two way street.

It is much easier for me to draw near to God knowing He enjoys my presence. In the past, when I drew near to God, I felt like the shy schoolboy tentatively moving in His direction, looking down, scuffing my shoes, afraid to meet His eyes. But then I looked up and saw that He was smiling.

This morning I was rereading the account of the return of the prodigal son. "I will arise and go to my father, and I will say to him, 'Father, I have sinned against heaven and before you. I am no longer worthy to be called your son. Treat me as one of your hired servants.' And he arose and came to his father. But while he was still a long way off, his father saw him and felt compassion, and ran and embraced him and kissed him. And the son said to him, 'Father, I have sinned against heaven and before you. I am no longer worthy to be called your son. But the father said to his servants, 'Bring quickly the best robe, and put it on him, and put a ring on his hand, and shoes on his feet. And bring the fattened calf and kill it, and let us eat and celebrate. For this my son was dead, and is alive again; he was lost, and is found.' And they began to celebrate." (Luke 15:18–24)

I love this picture of the Father who saw his son a long way off, had compassion, ran, embraced, and kissed his son. The son was trying to make his little speech of repentance, and his dad interrupted him, and grabbed him, and gave him a bear hug. This is our Dad too.

Another verse that may be descriptive of God giving us each a hug is found in Psalm 139:5. "You hem me in, behind and before, and lay your hand upon me." Whether this is accurate or not, in the past two years when I draw near to Him I have found that He is always smiling, always loving, and always welcoming.

Waiting and Being Still

A few years ago, I was a part of a small group working through the study materials for "Emotionally Healthy Spirituality" by Peter Scazzero. Each of us had daily assignments to fulfill, answering questions and looking up scripture. I found these easy to do. Before looking up verses and filling in the blanks, we were also instructed to be still for two minutes. Even though it was only a short time, I could not do it. Every Tuesday evening when we discussed the questions I had to humbly report that I had not been silent for two minutes. I fulfilled the rest of the assignment except for being quiet before God.

The next summer, Sandi and I were in the mountains and I rode my bike a few miles to a place overlooking the Delaware Water Gap called Lookout Point. I sat on a granite outcropping and for the first time, sat and drank in the presence of God. I talked a little, then listened, then simply enjoyed being in His presence. The best word to describe this new experience is "communing." I think I was there for the better part of an hour, then rode home.

The next day I rode over again, a little nervous, because what if God didn't meet me in such a deep and meaningful way like He had the day before. But God was faithful, and we had another time of communing and enjoying each other. This became a daily habit each afternoon through the end of the week. Sandi even became concerned about how long I was gone as the time grew to over an hour and longer. But time flew by for me, because I was with my Dad.

For decades God had met me when I was in a deep valley and cried out for help. I was recalling valley experiences from my past and it was enlightening to see how God faithfully showed up every time. I had an assurance God would help when I was at the end of my rope. I also knew He would answer my requests to bless the work I was doing, whether preaching, witnessing, or some other worthwhile Christian activity. But deep down I didn't believe He really enjoyed me or liked me if I was not engaged in seeking first the kingdom.

Why did it take two years after He had been at my side in my kitchen for me to experience this kind of fellowship? I think it is because it took me that long to really believe God liked me. It is not easy to wait on a God who you think is simply being kind, in a patronizing sort of way. But when you are assured and convinced in your heart that God truly likes you and enjoys spending time with you, then the relationship can move to a deeper level. God is not just there when I need Him, but I can enjoy His person and fellowship anytime, even without a reason.

Later that fall, we were back in the area and I couldn't wait to ride to the Lookout. I put on a jacket and a hat because it was breezy with a significant wind chill. I didn't have the proper gear and after a short pedal, was tempted to turn around and go back to our warm house, but then I remembered, I was going to meet my Dad. I kept pedaling. I didn't stay as long as in the summer, but God drew near to me, as I drew near to Him. God is always outside the door patiently waiting for me to open the door and invite Him to spend time with me. But I have to invite Him and let Him in. He is gentle and does not barge in or force His way. But when we seek Him, we do find Him.

Let God Enjoy You

Recently on an evening walk, I sensed God was enjoying our communion. He was happy being together, with me. I began smiling, for this was new territory in our relationship. I have trouble conceiving of coming before the King of Kings and Lord of Lords, then sitting down just to be together. I thought you came in to the King to report on your activity or make a petition.

But when I consider the goodness of God and the wonder of the gospel, since He loves us and likes us, does it not also follow for Him to enjoy us?

I am beginning to comprehend more of the glory and uniqueness of our Dad. For He is Immanuel, our God who chooses to be "with us". Ponder these passages:

"The LORD takes pleasure in his people; he adorns the humble with salvation." (Psalm 149:4)

"For you make him most blessed forever; you make him glad with the joy of your presence." (Psalm 21:6)

When I think about the account of the prodigal son returning home, I know of the joy of the Father is seeing His son who was lost, come home again. But then I began thinking about the banquet that evening. As the evening went on, I can see the young son, clothed, eating, and happy to be back. I also see the Dad, sitting near His son, not saying much, just reveling in the presence of His boy. Then occasionally their eyes would meet and nothing needed to be said, for they were connected, they were together again.

"The LORD takes pleasure in his people;" (Psalm 149:4)

Make a Start

If this call to open your heart and let God love you, resonates with you, may I encourage you to begin small. Aim for one minute reading or listening to the word, and one minute being still and communing with the living God. Give God a chance to talk to you. God is alive. He is near. He is real. He knows how to uniquely communicate to each one of His children, for He knows us better than we know ourselves.

"Seek the LORD while he may be found; call upon him while he is near;" (Isaiah 55:6)

"Glory in his holy name; let the hearts of those who seek the LORD rejoice! Seek the LORD and his strength; seek his presence continually!" (1Chronicles 16:10-11)

Prayer

Thank you for drawing near to us when we draw near to you. Thank you for patiently and faithfully knocking at the door of our innermost being. Thank you for speaking to us and inviting us to share a meal with you. Help us to trust You and open ourselves to your love and presence.

QUESTIONS FOR REFLECTION

1. What three examples from Scripture does Steve use when describing God's love? Name the Scripture reference and answer these questions: who, where, what is being said and/or done, and what is the significance?

2. How do you feel when you draw near to God? Do you see him smiling? If not, ask the Good Spirit to reveal why, and show you more about how God feels toward you.

3. If you have a story about communing with God, share it here in a few sentences or a paragraph.

4. Why did Steve have difficulty waiting on God, enjoying His presence, and communing with Him?

5. Do you enjoy the prospect of being still and letting God love you?

CHAPTER 13: GOD IS TREATING YOU AS SONS

When I began asking God to help me love Him in 2009, I had no idea how He would sovereignly answer this request. On the one hand, I have documented wonderful revelations I was given by the Spirit of God and through the word of God. On the other hand, I also went through the deepest valley I have ever known and experienced pain and crisis to a degree I would not wish on anyone. This is documented in another book entitled *"Crisis to Christ."*

But without both of what I call the blessing and the chastening, I would not be where I am today or be who I am. I am now able to truly give thanks in all that transpired, the good and the hard. For God is Lord of all and He has divinely orchestrated the whole symphony.

While this is the shortest chapter in the book, it provides insight into the way God loves His children. God is our Dad; which we have established. We are adopted children of God and His Spirit bears witness with our spirit we are His kids. We are loved with an everlasting love. He cannot stop loving us, because love is who He is. God is love. These are the foundation truths upon which our relationship is built.

Even Jesus was chastened and learned from His Father. "In the days of his flesh, Jesus offered up prayers and supplications, with loud cries and tears, to him who was able to save him from death, and he was heard because of his reverence. Although he was a son, he learned obedience through what he suffered. And being made perfect, he became the source of eternal salvation to all who obey him," (Hebrews 5:7–9)

As children of God we can also expect to be disciplined, chastised, and trained. When life is hard, it does not mean God is displeased with us, perhaps it is simply training and discipline. I am learning to see chastening as another way God reveals His love. I will let the scriptures speak for themselves in two renderings of the same passage in Hebrews 12:4–11. The first is from the English Standard Version (ESV) and the second from **The Message** by Eugene H. Peterson.

ESV

"In your struggle against sin you have not yet resisted to the point of shedding your blood. And have you forgotten the exhortation that addresses you as sons? 'My son, do not regard lightly the discipline of the Lord, nor be weary when reproved by him. For the Lord disciplines the one He loves, and chastises every son whom He receives.'

It is for discipline that you have to endure. God is treating you as sons. For what son is there whom his father does not discipline? If you are left without discipline, in which all have participated, then you are illegitimate children and not sons. Besides this, we have had earthly fathers who disciplined us and we respected them. Shall we not much more be subject to the Father of spirits and live? For they disciplined us for a short time as it seemed best to them, but he disciplines us for our good, that we may share his holiness. For the moment all discipline seems painful rather than pleasant, but later it yields the peaceful fruit of righteousness to those who have been trained by it."

The Message

"In this all-out match against sin, others have suffered far worse than you, to say nothing of what Jesus went through—all that bloodshed! So don't feel sorry for yourselves. Or have you forgotten how good parents treat children, and that God regards you as his children?

My dear child, don't shrug off God's discipline, but don't be crushed by it either. It's the child He loves that He disciplines; the child He embraces, He also corrects.

God is educating you; that's why you must never drop out. He's treating you as dear children. This trouble you're in isn't punishment; it's training, the normal experience of children. Only irresponsible parents leave children to fend for themselves. Would you prefer an irresponsible God? We respect our own parents for training and not spoiling us, so why not embrace God's training so we can truly live? While we were children, our parents did what seemed best to them. But God is doing what is best for us, training us to live God's holy best. At the time, discipline isn't much fun. It always feels like it's going against the grain. Later, of course, it pays off handsomely, for it's the well-trained who find themselves mature in their relationship with God."

Our Dad doesn't have any Baggage

Our Father God is a perfect parent. As a dad I have often disciplined out of anger or when I was upset. I was an imperfect Dad who regularly had to ask forgiveness of my children when I made mistakes in judgment or discipline. God knows everything. He is fully informed, completely loving, totally just, and incredibly merciful as He chastens us for our good. He is also with us as we are being chastened. "In all their affliction he was afflicted, and the angel of his presence saved them; in his love and in his pity he redeemed them; he lifted them up and carried them all the days of old." (Isaiah 63:9)

We have a sugar coated unbiblical view of love if we think God simply gives us lollipops all day to show that He cares for us. God is all wise, all knowing, and all loving. When He disciplines us, it is for our good. Here are a few more verses affirming the love of God for those experiencing His loving discipline.

"Those whom I love, I reprove and discipline, so be zealous and repent." (Revelation 3:19)

"Before I was afflicted I went astray, but now I keep your word." (Psalm 119:67)

"It is good for me that I was afflicted; that I may learn your statutes." (Psalm 119:71)

"Know then in your heart that, as a man disciplines his son, the Lord your God disciplines you." (Deuteronomy 8:5)

Prayer

Thank you for treating us as sons. Thank you for afflictions, reproof, chastening, training, and discipline. Thank you for being a responsible, committed, loving Dad.

QUESTIONS FOR REFLECTION

1. Steve shares that on the other side of the deepest valley he has ever known, he is able to give thanks in all things regarding that experience, because "God is Lord of all and He has divinely orchestrated the whole symphony." Think about the valleys you've traveled in your journey. Is there one in which you can look back on with thanksgiving, knowing God did a good work in you?

2. What word or phrase drew your attention as you read Hebrews 12:4–11 in the ESV and The Message?

3. Why does that phrase strike a chord in your spirit? Unpack your thoughts, and record them, as much as you are able.

4. Can you connect with the image of God as Father? Do you believe He disciplines us in love and for our good?

5. In what ways is this possible or not possible for you to believe in your life right now? Explain why.

CHAPTER 14: POSSIBLY THE MOST IMPORTANT CHAPTER

The central message from God's heart to us is He loves us. He has always loved us. When we were in a dark hopeless place, God the Father sent His Son Jesus to reacquaint us with this eternal message. When Jesus bore our sins on the cross, a way was made for us to have our sins removed and be close to God now and for eternity. We call this the Good News.

I have said this before but would like to restate it afresh. Not understanding the completeness of the gospel, and not being rooted and grounded in God's love contributed greatly to my crisis in 2012. Understanding grace and the good news more fully and being rooted and grounded in the knowledge God knows me, loves me, and likes me, has made me feel as if I have been born again, again. This is God's message and it is becoming mine. The knowledge and comprehension of the good news has changed my life and I believe it will continue to change the world, one heart at a time.

Understanding I do not have to accomplish things to please God because I am already pleasing in Christ makes a huge difference in allowing me to rest and not be driven. Knowing I am liked for who I am, by one who knows me intimately, frees me to be real and be myself and not work so hard to project an image of a successful man. But I still have a past with all the hurts, wounds, failures, disappointments, unfulfilled dreams, and sadness we have all experienced. Until I was convinced of God's love for me, I was unable to face and reflect on the pain I carry.

Not By Works

Up until 2012, I knew God could and would forgive my sin because of the death of Jesus on the cross. I simply needed to ask Him and believe Him. My past sins would be erased, I would have a blank slate, and it would be my joy and challenge to seek first and extend the Kingdom. In 1974, when I said, "Okay God, here we go," I threw myself into doing the work of God. People who know me recognize I have only two speeds, run and sleep.

These words describe my life as a zealous believer, "Do all the good you can. By all the means you can. In all the ways you can. In all the places you can. At all the times you can. To all the people you can. As long as ever you can." (This quote is mistakenly attributed to John Wesley.) Regardless of who said it, I believe this is a wonderful mindset to have, but only if I am being led by the Spirit.

After almost 40 years of living this way, I sat in our home that day in the spring and heard my wife tell me I couldn't do enough to please God. I don't know if I was always this driven, but this was certainly my life now. I did not understand the impact of the finished work of Christ on my behalf. I did not know I was already pleasing to God. I now believe that in Christ I am not only forgiven, I am also well pleasing, for Jesus is well pleasing and I am in Him.

In reading the letter to the Galatians, I discovered I am not the only one who believes in a form of "works" to be pleasing to God. It seems this tendency to begin with grace and then move to works is endemic to Christians and is addressed by Paul when writing to these believers. "For freedom Christ has set us free; stand firm therefore, and do not submit again to a yoke of slavery. Look: I, Paul, say to you that if you accept circumcision, Christ will be of no advantage to you. I testify again to every man who accepts circumcision that he is obligated to keep the whole law. You are severed from Christ, you who would be justified by the law; you have fallen away from grace. For through the Spirit, by faith, we ourselves eagerly wait for the hope of righteousness. For in Christ Jesus neither circumcision nor uncircumcision counts for anything, but only faith working through love. You were running well. Who hindered you from obeying the truth? This persuasion is not from him who calls you." (Galatians 5:1-8)

I believed salvation was by grace, but sanctification was by works. I felt like the more I did for God, and the better husband and father I became, the more God would love and smile upon me. Finally, my courageous wife sat down with me, and said, "You can't do enough to please God and you are hurting our family." I was wearing myself thin, and not on unprofitable pursuits. I was spending my energies on my wife, my family, church involvement, the business and ministry. I was pouring out in every direction, and had very little energy left. Our family paid the price of having a fragile husband and father who lived with condemnation for years, believing he did not measure up.

When we hear the Gospel for the first time, we begin with "Just as I am, without one plea," but then subtly begin to move towards "Trust and Obey for there is no other way to be happy in Jesus," as if we have to do something to earn God's favor. Sincere, earnest, believing Christians need to be continually reminded that salvation is always a gift. It is received and never earned. The summer of 2012 I comprehended in a deeper way the good news that I measured up because of what He did for me. I would like to say all was rosy from this point on, but it takes time and intentional study of the truth to undo decades of faulty thinking. Change may happen quickly in the heart, but lasting transformation and renewal transpire over time in the mind. I am still devoting hours every week to reprogramming old, default, unhealthy patterns of thinking and walking in the newness and freedom the truth brings.

Condemnation

Over the years I had lost the original sense of the nearness of God and distance had crept undetected in our relationship. I never articulated or stopped to think what I felt, I just kept my nose to the grindstone and sought to always be working to seek first and extend the kingdom. At the same time I knew God loved the world, so He must love me. My unspoken conviction was He loved me more if I did more for Him and I felt, as Sandi had described me, that I could never do enough to please God. By never thinking I could do enough, I felt I did not measure up and if I let myself think these unhealthy thoughts, could quickly be discouraged. I would describe this condition as a form of condemnation, which is radically different than conviction.

Conviction is from God and is a result of the work of the Holy Spirit in our hearts when we sin. While unpleasant, it is infused with hope, for we know when we confess our sin, He will forgive and restore us. Conviction is both painful and encouraging at the same time. "I tell you the truth: it is to your advantage that I go away, for if I do not go away, the Helper will not come to you. But if I go, I will send Him to you. And when He comes, He will convict the world concerning sin and righteousness and judgment." (John 16:7-8)

Condemnation is the is the debilitating, discouraging, life-crushing work of the "accuser of the brethren," which leads to despair, and is from the pit of hell. "The accuser of our brothers has been thrown down, who accuses them day and night before our God." (Revelation 12:10) When I am experiencing condemned, I am tempted to lose hope and give up altogether.

In the Gospels we have an amazing example of two men who exemplify the extreme difference between conviction and condemnation. Peter sinned when he denied Jesus, was convicted, and wept bitterly. Miraculously he was forgiven, restored, and became a leader in the early church. Judas betrayed Jesus, regretted his actions, also wept, gave back the money, confessed his sin, but gave in to despair and hung himself.

Peter is an example of Godly grief, or conviction. He was convicted of his sin and with the help of God, found hope and restoration. He sinned grievously three times in one night and later affirmed he loved Jesus three times in one day.

I don't know what went on in the heart and mind of Judas but his condition seems to embody someone who is living with condemnation, or a form of worldly grief. 2 Corinthians 7:10 describes both concepts, "For Godly grief produces a repentance that leads to salvation without regret, whereas worldly grief produces death."

I have lived in a state of semi-condemnation by not feeling like I could do enough, or be enough, to please God. Understanding the scope of the life and death of Jesus, and the subsequent gifts of forgiveness and righteousness, has helped me overcome condemnation in a new way. Thank God that, "There is therefore now no condemnation for those who are in Christ Jesus. For the law of the Spirit of life has set you free in Christ Jesus from the law of sin and death." (Romans 8:1-2)

Shame

I know my sins are forgiven and I am no longer guilty, because of Jesus. I have just explored condemnation, which I think is the Achilles heel of many earnest Christians. Those disciples who are most concerned about living a life which is pleasing to God are the same ones who are the most susceptible to condemnation.

Shame is universal and not restricted to devout believers. Everyone experiences shame, fears shame, and does all in their power to avoid it. Guilt seems to be the result of something we have done. It is an action outside of ourselves. Even though I sinned, it is at arm's length.

Shame is not as much about what I did, as who I am. Shame is an attack on my identity and is much more deadly. Guilt says I did a bad thing, shame says I am a bad person. Guilt stains the hands, shame stains the soul. When I made mistakes as a child, I remember being told I could 'wreck a free lunch' or 'mess up a one car funeral.' This words hurt then and now I recognize it is because I was being told I had not only done a dumb thing, I was dumb. Perhaps this is why I have trouble believing I am loved unconditionally by God or my family.

The fearful component of shame is being seen, known, and exposed. We all dread being fully naked and bare before others. But God knows us as no one else, He created us in His image, and with full knowledge He chooses to love and like us. When we give place to shame we have difficulty believing this incredible truth. I am fully persuaded God loves my wife and children and many other brothers and sisters in Christ. My struggle is to believe He also loves me. Unfortunately I give credence to the lie that if He really knew me, He wouldn't love me.

Just verbalizing the problem makes me realize how silly and sad this argument is, yet it has crippled me and kept me from living and tasting an abundant life for decades. God not only loves us, He genuinely likes us. He knows each of us intimately. He formed us in our mother's womb. The Holy Spirit spoke through David these incredible inspired and eternal words:

"O Lord, you have searched me and known me! You formed my inward parts; you knitted me together in my mother's womb. My frame was not hidden from you, when I was being made in secret, intricately woven in the depths of the earth. Your eyes saw my unformed substance; in your book were written, every one of them, the days that were formed for me, when as yet there was none of them. How precious to me are your thoughts, O God! How vast is the sum of them! If I would count them, they are more than the sand. I awake, and I am still with you." (Psalms 139:1, 13, 15–18)

He was at His Best When I was at My Worst

Jesus was sent to die for me when I was in the worst possible condition. He knew my sins and my propensity for sin, and loved me still. "God shows his love for us in that while we were still sinners,

Christ died for us." (Romans 5:8) Even when He was crucified, He did not change His mind, but loved us to the end, saying, "Father forgive them for they know not what they do." (Luke 23:34)

This kind of love which is all knowing, all forgiving, and unchanging is amazing. It is perfect love, and it removes and casts out all fear. "There is no fear in love, but perfect love casts out fear." (1 John 4:18)

It is the love of Jesus for me which covers a multitude of sin and leaves me clean, fresh, and forgiven. "Above all, keep loving one another earnestly, since love covers a multitude of sins." (1 Peter 4:8) Jesus has loved me completely, perfectly, and covered all of my sins.

Whether my problem is with guilt, condemnation, shame or some other obstacle, I am convinced God has the solution and it will be found in Jesus and the truth of God's word. Peter pens these wonderful words of assurance: "His divine power has granted to us all things that pertain to life and Godliness." (2 Peter 1:3) If some new attack of the deceiver emerges, I will bring it to God, ask Him for the solution and gain new insight as He opens my eyes to some new facet of grace I haven't tapped into yet. The Gospel covers any and all obstacles to new life in Jesus the Christ.

Paul says he is not ashamed of the Gospel for, "It is the power of God for salvation to everyone who believes." (Romans 1:16) Hearing the good news of the Gospel and deepening our understanding of it, releases the power of God in our lives leading to real change. We all need to continually and regularly hear and comprehend the Gospel.

I had the opportunity to hear Dutch Christian, Holocaust survivor, Corrie ten Boom, speak in the 1970s. You may think she would have been teaching about life in a concentration camp, or how God enabled her to forgive the German guard who made her life miserable. I was surprised to learn one of her main themes was the simple gospel of how God forgives our sins. She would say, with her Dutch accent, something like this: "God forgives your sins and casts them into the ocean of His love, and then puts up a sign that says 'No Fishing.'" She was referencing Psalms 103:12 "As far as the east is from the west, so far does He remove our transgressions from us." The evening I heard her speak, she was addressing a predominantly Christian audience. Regardless of how long we have believed in Jesus, followers of Christ need to be reminded often of the forgiveness of Christ.

Gospel Centered

Over the past two years I have addressed thousands of earnest believers and have found most of them do not believe, in their innermost heart, that God loves them, likes them, and is pleased with them. As a result we are crippled in our ability to give and receive love, which is the heart of the matter. I have lived in a state of semi-condemnation for years and do not plan on returning, instead I have moved my tent and am diligently working to abide in His love.

I believe God wants us to "know" of His affection. I believe God wants us to have "life abundantly" that "our joy may be full." I am also convinced we have an enemy who came to steal, kill, and destroy what God desires to give us. "The thief comes only to steal and kill and destroy. I came that they may have life and have it abundantly. (John 10:10)

Thankfully, "He who is in you is greater than He who is in the world." (1 John 4:4)

"So we have come to know and to believe the love that God has for us. God is love, and whoever abides in love abides in God, and God abides in him." (1 John 4:16)

"Until now you have asked nothing in my name. Ask, and you will receive, that your joy may be full." (John 16:24)

We Have an Enemy

Paul says he is not "ignorant of the devices of our enemy." (2 Corinthians 2:11) The devil is not a creator, but a liar, robber, and deceiver. Our battle is a spiritual one. "For though we walk in the flesh, we are not waging war according to the flesh. For the weapons of our warfare are not of the flesh but have divine power to destroy strongholds. We destroy arguments and every lofty opinion raised against the knowledge of God, and take every thought captive to obey Christ." (2 Corinthians 10:3-5)

God came to give us abundant life, the devil tries to take it away (John 10:10). If our enemy can't keep us from choosing life, following Jesus, and being born from above, then he undertakes to steal our new life, with blatant attacks of sin, or subtle attacks of guilt, condemnation, and shame. May God help us to recognize his dirty lies, reject them, and be set free from them. May He also enable us to grasp how much God knows us, sees us, loves us, likes us, for who we are and not based on what we do.

Appeal to the Spirit

When I don't know how to pray as I ought, I ask the Spirit for divine assistance. "In the same way, the Spirit helps us in our weakness. We do not know what we ought to pray for, but the Spirit Himself intercedes for us through wordless groans. And He who searches our hearts knows the mind of the Spirit, because the Spirit intercedes for God's people in accordance with the will of God." (Romans 8:26-27) I ask the Spirit for assistance. One more aspect of this multi-faceted member of the Trinity is that He knows how to fight. "If it is by the Spirit of God that I cast out demons, then the kingdom of God has come upon you." (Matthew 12:28) Jesus was helped to war in the Spirit.

I assume most believers have had some teaching on spiritual warfare from Ephesians. Paul exhorts us to put on the whole armor of God. Many years ago I used to consciously put on each of these divine armaments by faith each morning. I would visualize a point on each piece and trusted God to help me be strong in the Lord and in His armor.

"Be strong in the Lord and in the strength of His might. Put on the whole armor of God, that you may be able to stand against the schemes of the devil. For we do not wrestle against flesh and blood, but against the rulers, against the authorities, against the cosmic powers over this present darkness, against the spiritual forces of evil in the heavenly places. Therefore take up the whole armor of God, that you may be able to withstand in the evil day, and having done all, to stand firm. Stand therefore, having fastened on the belt of truth, and having put on the breastplate of righteousness, and, as shoes for your feet, having put on the readiness given by the gospel of peace. In all circumstances take up the shield of faith, with which you can extinguish all the flaming darts of the evil one; and take the helmet of salvation, and the sword of the Spirit, which is the word of God, praying at all times in the Spirit." (Ephesians 6:10-18)

The Sword of the Spirit, the Word of God

This book on the love of God has been rooted in scripture. Since we can expect to be attacked by our enemy we need to know the truth. The sword of the Spirit is one weapon. Three times in the gospel of Matthew, Jesus is tempted. Three times He responds, "It is written." When we are tempted to doubt the truth, feel discouraged, or are struggling to believe the good news, affirming the truth of scripture is a powerful antidote to attacks from the devil.

I don't always need to be clever when engaging in spiritual warfare, I simply need to put up a fight. When combatting lies and doubts which do not seem to give way, I pray, "In Jesus' name, I resist the devil." I can do this aloud or silently. I am not a fan of talking to the devil directly, instead I hide behind my big brother Jesus and pray in His name. "Submit yourselves therefore to God. Resist the devil, and he will flee from you. Draw near to God, and He will draw near to you." (James 4:7-8)

Obstacles and Antidotes

One Saturday last fall, Sandi, John and I were driving to attend our first college football game. Sandi and John were dozing while I drove through beautiful central Pennsylvania. As I admired the scenery I asked God why we have so much trouble apprehending His affection for us? The message being broadcast from heaven is clear and being sent out perfectly, but the reception on our end is garbled and misunderstood.

Many of these obstacles I have addressed throughout the book, but this is such a critical topic, a little repetition may help. Accompanying each obstacle is the truth to set us free from the lie.

Obstacle 1: I Feel Unworthy

Antidote: "The saying is trustworthy and deserving of full acceptance, that Christ Jesus came into the world to save sinners, of whom I am the foremost." (1 Timothy 1:15)

"I have not come to call the righteous but sinners to repentance." (Luke 5:32)

"God shows his love for us in that while we were still sinners, Christ died for us." (Romans 5:8)

Obstacle 2: Unbelief

Antidote: "Faith comes from hearing, and hearing through the word of Christ." (Romans 10:17)

"I do believe, but help me overcome my unbelief!" (Mark 9:24 NLT)

Obstacle 3: My secret sins disqualify me.

Antidote: "O LORD, you have searched me and known me! You know when I sit down and when I rise up; you discern my thoughts from afar. You search out my path and my lying down and are acquainted with all my ways." (Psalm 139:1–3)

If I say, 'Surely the darkness shall cover me, and the light about me be night,' even the darkness is not dark to you; the night is bright as the day, for darkness is as light with you." (Psalm 139:11–12)

Obstacle 4: My nature and character are flawed.

Antidote: "Everyone who calls upon the name of the Lord shall be saved." (Acts 2:21)

"For you formed my inward parts; you knitted me together in my mother's womb. I praise you, for I am fearfully and wonderfully made. Wonderful are your works; my soul knows it very well. My frame was not hidden from you, when I was being made in secret, intricately woven in the depths of the earth." (Psalm 139:13–15)

Obstacle 5: He loves others, but no me.

Antidote: "The true light, which gives light to everyone, was coming into the world. He was in the world, and the world was made through him, yet the world did not know him. He came to his own, and his own people did not receive him. But to all who did receive him, who believed in his name, he gave the right to become children of God, who were born, not of blood nor of the will of the flesh nor of the will of man, but of God." (John 1:9–13)

"This is good, and it is pleasing in the sight of God our Savior, who desires all people to be saved and to come to the knowledge of the truth. For there is one God, and there is one mediator between God and men, the man Christ Jesus, who gave himself as a ransom for all, which is the testimony given at the proper time." (1 Timothy 2:3–6)

Obstacle 6: I'm afraid to open up and receive God's kindness and love.

Antidote: "There is no fear in love, but perfect love casts out fear." (1 John 4:18)

Obstacle 7: I don't measure up. I will never be enough.

Antidote: "For by grace you have been saved through faith. And this is not your own doing; it is the gift of God, not a result of works" (Ephesians 2:8–9)

Obstacle 8: I am not deserving of such love.

Antidote: "The wages of sin is death, but the

free gift of God is eternal life in Christ Jesus our Lord." (Romans 6:23)

Obstacle 9: I haven't done enough good works.

Antidote: "He saved us, not because of works done by us in righteousness, but according to his own mercy, by the washing of regeneration and renewal of the Holy Spirit," (Titus 3:5)

None of these articulated obstacles, or enemies, are able to keep us from being loved, only our own stuff. Paul was convinced and I hope God, by His Spirit and through His inspired word, will convince each of us as well. "For I am convinced that nothing can ever separate us from God's love. Neither death nor life, neither angels nor demons, neither our fears for today nor our worries about tomorrow—not even the powers of hell can separate us from God's love. No power in the sky above or in the earth below—indeed, nothing in all creation will ever be able to separate us from the love of God that is revealed in Christ Jesus our Lord." (Romans 8:38–39 NLT)

Prayer

Thank You for "the gospel, for it is the power of God for salvation to everyone who believes, to the Jew first and also to the Greek." (Romans 1:16) May we "have strength to comprehend with all the saints what is the breadth and length and height and depth, and to know the love of Christ that surpasses knowledge, that (we) may be filled with all the fullness of God. (Ephesians 3:18–19)

QUESTIONS FOR REFLECTION

1. What is the impact of the finished work of Christ on your behalf? Or, another way to say it, how does the Good News affect you on a daily basis? See if you can write a summary of the Gospel in your own words (try to avoid "Scripture-ese"!☺

2. Think about your Christian life. Are there one or more things you think you HAVE to do, for God to accept and like you? Dig deep. There might be more of this under the surface than you realize.

3. Describe the difference between conviction and condemnation. Which do you feel more often? Why?

4. Describe the difference between guilt and shame. How does Satan use lies to crush and cripple people under feelings of shame? If you struggle with feelings of shame, meditate and ponder the truths of Psalm 139.

5. What are some ways you can "work diligently to abide in His love"? How do we engage in spiritual warfare with the devil?

CHAPTER 15: WHY KNOWING GOD'S LOVE IS IMPORTANT

You may have heard it said that you cannot give what you do not have. In the same way, I hope it is evident that we are unable to love until we have first been loved. This is an eternal verity that is plainly taught in scripture. Love begets love. The following three verses are all found in 1 John 4, but I have taken the liberty of reordering them:

"We love because he first loved us." (1 John 4:19)

"In this is love, not that we have loved God but that He loved us and sent His Son to be the propitiation for our sins." (1 John 4:10)

"We have come to know and to believe the love that God has for us. God is love, and whoever abides in love abides in God, and God abides in him." (1 John 4:16)

God always makes the first move, and His strategy works. John knew he was loved. His name even means "beloved." His letter is written to a church who were convinced God was for them.

This chapter is about the fruit of believing that you are loved and liked by God. What does it look like to know this truth deep in our souls, and how, practically speaking, would our lives change if we completely and stubbornly believed it?

Four Wonderful Fruits

I. When we know we are loved by God, we are able to love God, which is our primary responsibility. "You shall love the Lord your God with all your heart and with all your soul and with all your mind. This is the great and first commandment." (Matthew 22:37–38)

II. When we know we are loved we are empowered to practice the new commandment. "A new commandment I give to you, that you love one another: just as I have loved you" (John 13:34)

III. When husbands know they are loved, they can fulfill the call of God to "love their wives as Christ loved the church." (Ephesians 5:25)

IV. When fathers and mothers know they are unconditionally loved, they are equipped to love their children unconditionally as they "bring them up in the discipline and instruction of the Lord." (Ephesians 6:4)

Any one of these fruits is worth the effort to pursue God until He makes you know you are loved and liked. I first embarked on this journey because of the deficiencies in my own relationship with God.

I can now say my Heavenly Dad and I are tight in a way I did not dare to hope for or believe. I love God more than I ever have. I have found out He genuinely likes me. I believe I am created with an eternal longing in my heart for God alone. Nothing else will satisfy the deep desire of my heart to be fully known and fully loved by God. I was made by Him and for Him when "He put eternity" into my heart. (Ecclesiastes 3:11)

I used to be motivated by fear – fear of not being accepted, fear of not belonging, fear of not measuring up. I was motivated to earn love, to prove myself worthy of love. Now I am motivated because I am loved. I am not driven by fear, and I am experiencing the truth of 1 John 4:18, "There is no fear in love, but perfect love casts out fear." I can also identify with the Apostle Paul, who was motivated and controlled by love, and not by doubt and anxiety. "For the love of Christ controls us." (2 Corinthians 5:14)

Knowing I am an adopted child of God has drastically changed my relationship with the people who are nearest and dearest to my heart, my wife and sons. It was the fear of losing them which drove me to get the help I needed. Not only are these precious people still close to me, our love for each other has grown and deepened. Having my identity in Christ alone, and not in my work, or how good of a husband or Dad I was, has freed me up to be more real, authentic, and transparent.

This next statement may seem a little strange, but give me some space please. I no longer need my children to like me or depend on me. For most of my life I needed to be needed. I wanted to be liked. Now I am seeking to live vertically, looking to God alone to be my compass and motivation. As I am aware of being liked by God I am more free to be who God designed me to be. God is helping me to be more fully present and open. I am able to value and articulate my emotions, instead of dismissing them. When looking to God alone for acceptance and identity, I don't depend, in an unhealthy way, on my wife or our children for my own emotional needs to be met. God likes me for who I am and not for what I do. This is a simple sentence, but far reaching in its implications.

I am a much better communicator. I can hear, and receive information without reacting as emotionally as I have in the past or taking what is said to me as personally as I once did. I am not perfect, but have made big strides. For most of my life, it was extremely difficult to respond thoughtfully when I was taking all input personally. Now, I am finding I have a greater freedom to hear and speak the truth in love. In the past I was not "sensitive;" I was simply not rooted and grounded in the love of God and took what was said as a threat to my identity.

When I am investing in my connection with heaven, dealing with my own pain, and establishing Godly boundaries, my home is a safer place. I am nicer to be around. Our family has better conversations. We can even hold differing opinions and still love each other. All of my sons are free to join different churches and hold to a variety of theologies and still be accepted at our dinner table. When I was not as rooted in the love of God as I am now, life was more black and white. I had strong convictions of what was biblical, what music was helpful, and what churches were acceptable. It is not wrong to have strong convictions, but it is wrong to impose them "ex cathedra," authoritatively, on your family. When I did not have as healthy a sense of my identity in Christ, I was unable to entertain opposition or have a reasonable conversation with those who disagreed with my positions. According to Paul in Romans 14, I believe we should all have convictions, but also treat each other with respect and give grace to one another. These are new skills I am learning. "One person esteems one day as better than another, while another esteems all days alike. Each one should be fully convinced in his own mind. (Romans 14:5) "Therefore let us not pass judgment on one another any longer, but rather decide never to put a stumbling block or hindrance in the way of a brother." (Romans 14:13)

When rooted and grounded, I am able to face my own stuff, explore the sources of my own pain, and ask God to search my heart. The more grounded I am in God, the more I am able to work through these unpleasant forays into my own baggage. If I don't deal with my stuff, I know eventually it will impact my relationship with those who are closest to me. I think of my stuff as radioactive waste, stored in lead suitcases, hidden in the corner of my closet. As long as life is smooth sailing, the containers remain safe and sealed. When my buttons are pushed, or when I am tired, stressed, or overworked, then the harmful waste begins to seep out of the container and contaminates the other people in my life. My wife and children have paid the price for pain I had not acknowledged nor confronted. "Search me, O God, and know my heart! Try me and know my thoughts! And see if there be any 'way of pain' in me, and lead me in the way everlasting! (Psalms 139:23-24)

A word which has been bandied about for years, which I did not understand, is "boundaries." I never had them. I poured out in every direction and did not know how to say "No." I did not have time for Steve; I considered this selfish. A true disciple, I reasoned, would be always giving and seeking first the Kingdom of God. I see now this inability to love myself and take time to rest, be still, and develop my relationship with God, was harmful to myself and those around me. I don't know my own heart, but one thing I am learning, my Dad likes me just the way I am. His yoke is easy and His burden is light and doable. I take naps now. I go for walks. I am trying to develop some hobbies. I am learning to say "No," which is hard for me still. But I am making progress!

All of this sounds very lofty and spiritual, so let me make it a little more earthy. Since I know I am pleasing through Christ, I am able to not be continually stirring myself to do more, but am finding time for a good night's rest or a nap when I feel the need. With this extra energy, I am glad to help out with dishes, loading and unloading the dishwasher, and folding my laundry. A few weeks ago, my wife commented how attractive she found me while sorting and folding my clothes. Wee hoo!

These next few fruits may sound silly, but I do not get as angry with inanimate objects as in the past. I can recall many times when I would bump my head on a low doorway, or hit my thumb with a hammer, or stumble into a wall. Sad to say, I have cursed doorways, thrown hammers, and hit walls as if they were conspiring to make my life miserable. I later had to repair the wall, and the hammer may still be in the gutter of our previous home. I am not proud to write this, but when you work hard, and don't allow some time to rest, be refreshed, and allow yourself to build up an energy reserve, even hammers and walls can push your buttons. This has almost ceased. This is the good fruit of devoting time to resting in the Lord and in His word.

The more I am rooted in Christ, the greater capacity I have to walk in the moccasins of others. When I am anxious about my own standing with God, or not secure in who I am as an adopted child of God, I use up my energies working on pleasing

Him and not thinking of others. Now I am finding new abilities to listen to others, see life from their perspective, consider how my words might impact them, and develop strategies to build them up. This kind of awareness has not been on my front burner for a long time.

I have always wanted to be a mentor and father to my sons. I wish I could have a "do over" in that department. I devoted so much energy to just keeping my own nose clean and working on following Christ myself I was not as available to help my sons as I wish I had. I did what I could and gave the best I had, but I see now how different I would have been as a Dad, if I had the relationship with God then, I have now. I actually have something to offer now. Taking better care of myself has also enabled me to have more energy and time for what is really important. I think back to making a tent with my boys, and then falling asleep inside of it because I was always burning the candle at both ends. But God knows and He is a Redeemer. I can still be a Dad to my sons, and their kiddos. Maybe this is why grandpas are so nice! Too soon old and too late smart, as the Amish say.

Knowing God is for me has added a whole new dimension to my personal times with God. Without an obsession to work to be accepted and pleasing, I am learning to enjoy God. "Knowing God" is a precious fruit of "knowing God's love." God is so much more than a need-supplier or a sin-forgiver or a burden-bearer. He is good, really good. He is kind. He is patient. He is creative. He has a sense of humor. We enjoy being in each other's presence. I am finally getting to know my Dad for who He is and not only for what He can do for me.

Prayer

Father, fulfill this scripture in my heart, and in my family. "The LORD your God will circumcise your heart and the heart of your offspring, so that you will love the LORD your God with all your heart and with all your soul, that you may live." (Deuteronomy 30:6)

QUESTIONS FOR REFLECTION

1. What can "reset our motivation engine"?

2. Is there any person you depend on for your identity? What relationships or what job titles or functions is your identity based on?

3. Are you looking to someone or something to meet your emotional needs which only God can satisfy?

4. Which fruit that Steve experienced as he walked and lived in God's love would you like to experience more fully?

5. List as many fruits of Knowing God's Love, as you can from this chapter. After you are finished, go back and select the one you would like to experience more fully.

CHAPTER 16: THE KNOWLEDGE OF GOD

When my quest to love God began, I desired a relationship with God based on love and not duty. I wanted to love God and be loved by Him. As my journey has progressed I have found loving God is not the end of my pilgrimage but one more step towards knowing God. The more I know Him, the more I love and appreciate Him. This love is not solely based on what He has done for me, but is growing to encompass who He is.

Just as He loves us for who we are and not for what we have or have not done, so I am finding myself loving God because of who He is. His character, His nature, His attributes, are worth knowing, loving, and admiring. There is a song written by Bill Gaither which continues to come to mind called "The Longer I Serve Him." My heart resonates with the chorus: "The longer I serve Him, the sweeter He grows; The more that I love Him, more love He bestows."

Spirit and Truth

A few weeks ago I sensed God communicating the words "spirt and truth" to my heart. That phrase comes from the conversation between Jesus and the Samaritan woman at the well. "The hour is coming, and is now here, when the true worshipers will worship the Father in spirit and truth, for the Father is seeking such people to worship him. God is spirit, and those who worship him must worship in spirit and truth." (John 4:23-34)

"Spirit and Truth" are a call for me to not only spend time in the Bible (the truth) but deepen my connection with the living God, for God is Spirit. Since I received these words, I have continued to read the Bible daily, and then give equal time investing in my relationship with the living God.

My new routine begins with time in the word, as I have been doing for years. Since 1976 I have made a habit of reading scripture daily, compassing the Bible from Genesis to Revelation once each year. I find my heart is softened as I am exposed to the inspired passages. Anointed words of life are true heart food. My faith has also been increased for "faith comes from hearing, and hearing through the word of Christ." (Romans 10:17).

This quiet time is followed by a walk. I find when I am sitting in my comfy chair early in the morning, I am prone to drowsiness and distraction. When I walk (also a good source of exercise) I am able to focus my attention on communing with God alone. My heart and spirit are encouraged in this precious time with the living God for "the Spirit gives life." (2 Corinthians 3:6).

I like the word communing for sometimes I talk, other times I listen. This past week I prayed the prayer found several times in Revelation, "Give me ears to hear 'what the Spirit says'" (Revelation 2:11, 2:17, ...) God faithfully meets me as I seek Him. As a result of these times, walking with God I find myself growing and worshiping in "spirit and truth."

Reading scripture increases my knowledge "about" God, communing daily is increasing my knowledge "of" God, or as Peter exhorts, "grow in the grace and knowledge of our Lord and Savior Jesus Christ." (2 Peter 3:18)

While attending seminary I had the opportunity to rent a room in the home of Elisabeth Elliot. By interacting with her on a daily basis, eating meals, doing chores, attending church together, I got to know her as a person, and not a famous speaker and author. Now, when I read her books or listen to a recorded talk, I receive so much more from what she says because I recognize her voice and know her heart.

The God in the Bible, is my Dad. He is alive. I enjoy spending time learning about Him in the past, and I am so grateful for opportunities to experience His presence in the present. My reading of the written word is enhanced by knowing the living word.

If you have been reading these newsletters or heard me speak in the past, you know I have been unable to "wait on God" for I had difficulty believing His grace and how much He truly cared for me. It is only in the past few years I am finally convinced God not only loves me, but likes me. I think if He had whispered "spirt and truth" five years ago I would not have known how to respond. For while I knew much about scripture I was deficient in my daily relationship with my God.

Believing God is beaming when I draw near to Him makes it so much easier to approach Him. I know He not only loves me, but genuinely enjoys my company. He is my Dad. He knows me intimately and still affectionately desires hanging out with me. I know this from the source of truth, the holy scripture, which says "God is for me" (Psalm 56:9) and Jesus said, "As the Father has loved me, so have I loved you." (John 15:9)

David certainly had a wonderful connection with the Almighty. "Oh, taste and see that the Lord is good! Blessed is the man who takes refuge in him!" (Psalms 34:8) His inspired words encourage me to move beyond seeing God from afar, but getting close while tasting His goodness.

I have also thought about other passages which point to the life-giving nature of the Spirit of God.

"It is the Spirit who gives life; the flesh is no help at all. The words that I have spoken to you are spirit and life." (John 6:63)

"The Spirit of God has made me, and the breath of the Almighty gives me life." (Job 33:4)

The Love of Christ Controls Us

Paul zealously pursued the establishment of the church. He passionately fought for the truth and endured unbelievable hardships for the brethren. But his love for God was his primary motivation. "I am hard pressed between the two. My desire is to depart and be with Christ, for that is far better. But to remain in the flesh is more necessary on your account." (Philippians 1:23-24) His desire was not only to see the body of Christ established, but to know Christ. "For the love of Christ controls us." (2 Corinthians 5:14)

In Philippians 3, Paul bares his soul and reveals his all consuming ambition. "Whatever gain I had, I counted as loss for the sake of Christ. Indeed, I count everything as loss because of the surpassing worth of knowing Christ Jesus my Lord. For his sake I have suffered the loss of all things and count them as rubbish, in order that I may gain Christ and be found in him, not having a righteousness of my own that comes from the law, but that which comes through faith in Christ, the righteousness from God that depends on faith— that I may know him." (Philippians 3:7-10)

Just as Paul was instrumental in establishing the church, Moses was the chosen instrument of God to form the nation of Israel. At one juncture, Moses offered to have his own name blotted out of the book of life in exchange for the redemption of Israel. He loved his people. What ultimately motivated Moses was his love for God and his desire to know Him.

"Now therefore, if I have found favor in your sight, please show me now your ways, that I may know you." (Exodus 33:13) Moses sought to see and understand God's ways so he might learn more about God's person. Paul, Moses, Abraham, Joseph, Samuel, and David shared one common purpose, a desire to know God. These chosen few were wonderfully anointed to do the work of God, but the shared desire of their innermost being, was their love for God.

"Thus says the Lord: 'Let not the wise man boast in his wisdom, let not the mighty man boast in his might, let not the rich man boast in his riches, but let him who boasts boast in this, that he understands and knows me, that I am the Lord who practices steadfast love, justice, and righteousness in the earth. For in these things I delight, declares the Lord.'" (Jeremiah 9:23)

Hosea proclaims "Let us know; let us press on to know the Lord; his going out is sure as the dawn; he will come to us as the showers, as the spring rains that water the earth." (Hosea 6:3)

Jesus declared "And this is eternal life, that they know you the only true God, and Jesus Christ whom you have sent." (John 17:3)

I have a dream. I am looking forward to the day when followers of Jesus gather to talk about and ponder the attributes of God and what they have learned about Him and His character. These earnest meetings would be comprised of kindred spirits who share insights they have received from scripture as they have pressed on to know the Lord. They would tell of experiences they had when the presence of God was especially near. This would be true fellowship indeed.

This day is coming. According to Jeremiah 31, referenced in Hebrews 8:11–12, "They shall not teach, each one his neighbor and each one his brother, saying, 'Know the Lord,' for they shall all know me, from the least of them to the greatest. For I will be merciful toward their iniquities, and I will remember their sins no more."

May God turn us heavenward and give us hearts to know Him. "And I will give them a heart to know Me, for I am the Lord; and they will be My people, and I will be their God, for they will return to Me with their whole heart." (Jeremiah 24:7 NASB)

I hope as we seek to love God we will find our hearts satisfied with a new understanding and comprehension of His grace and His person. I hope our new experiences with God will improve our ability to love our spouse and family members as we have been loved. It is my prayer that the good Spirit of God will enable and inspire each of us to "press on to know the Lord." (Hosea 6:3)

God Pursues Us

"Surely your goodness and unfailing love will pursue me all the days of my life, and I will live in the house of the LORD forever." (Psalms 23:6 NLT) Remember where we began, "We love because He first loved us." (1 John 4:19) Earlier in the same chapter John writes, "This is real love—not that we loved God, but that he loved us and sent his Son as a sacrifice to take away our sins." (1 John 4:10 NLT)

God has taken the initiative to seek us, to pursue us, and to love us. Let's be assured of His affection and run to Him.

Prayer

"May the Lord direct your hearts to the love of God and to the steadfastness of Christ." (2 Thessalonians 3:5)

QUESTIONS FOR REFLECTION

1. Listen to your prayers. Are you more often thankful for what God does, or for who He is?

2. What motivated Paul, and Moses?

3. According to Jeremiah 9:23, what does God delight in?

4. What is Steve's dream for followers of Jesus?

5. Do you believe it is God's will for you to know in your heart of hearts that He loves and likes you for who you are? Then ask Him to write these truths on your heart, based on my favorite prayer scripture: "This is the confidence that we have toward him, that if we ask anything according to his will he hears us. And if we know that he hears us in whatever we ask, we know that we have the requests that we have asked of him." (1 John 5:14–15)

APPENDIX A
THE FATHER AND
THE SON

The Father has great joy in His Son

"Even as he spoke, a bright cloud overshadowed them, and a voice from the cloud said, 'This is my dearly loved Son, who brings me great joy.'" (John 17:5 NLT)

The Father loved the Son

"Father, I desire that they also, whom you have given me, may be with me where I am, to see my glory that you have given me because you loved me before the foundation of the world." (John 17:24)

The Father trusted His Son

"The Father loves the Son and has given all things into his hand." (John 3:35)

"All things have been handed over to me by my Father, and no one knows who the Son is except the Father, or who the Father is except the Son and anyone to whom the Son chooses to reveal him." (Luke 10:22)

The Father and the Son work together giving life

"For as the Father raises the dead and gives them life, so also the Son gives life to whom he will." (John 5:21)

God the Father Has given Jesus responsibility

"The Father judges no one, but has given all judgment to the Son, that all may honor the Son, just as they honor the Father. Whoever does not honor the Son does not honor the Father who sent him." (John 5:22–23)

God the Father and Jesus the Son had each other's back

"Yet even if I do judge, my judgment is true, for it is not I alone who judge, but I and the Father who sent me. In your Law it is written that the testimony of two people is true. I am the one who bears witness about myself, and the Father who sent me bears witness about me." (John 8:16–18)

Jesus came from the Father and is going to the Father

"I came from the Father and have come into the world, and now I am leaving the world and going to the Father." (John 16:28)

The Father sent His Son

"Jesus said to them again, 'Peace be with you. As the Father has sent me, even so I am sending you.'" (John 20:21)

The Father glorifies the Son

"Jesus answered, 'If I glorify myself, my glory is nothing. It is my Father who glorifies me, of whom you say, 'He is our God.' But you have not known him. I know him. If I were to say that I do not know him, I would be a liar like you, but I do know him and I keep his word.'" (John 8:54-55)

"When Jesus had spoken these words, he lifted up his eyes to heaven, and said, 'Father, the hour has come; glorify your Son that the Son may glorify you,'" (John 17:1)

The Father is with His Son

"Behold, the hour is coming, indeed it has come, when you will be scattered, each to his own home, and will leave me alone. Yet I am not alone, for the Father is with me." (John 16:32)

The Father and the Son were always together

"Father, glorify me in your own presence with the glory that I had with you before the world existed." (John 17:5)

The Father and Jesus are in unity

"If I am not doing the works of my Father, then do not believe me; but if I do them, even though you do not believe me, believe the works, that you may know and understand that the Father is in me and I am in the Father." (John 10:37-38)

"I am no longer in the world, but they are in the world, and I am coming to you. Holy Father, keep them in your name, which you have given me, that they may be one, even as we are one." (John 17:11)

The Father and the Son love us!

"O righteous Father, even though the world does not know you, I know you, and these know that you have sent me. I made known to them your name, and I will continue to make it known, that the love with which you have loved me may be in them, and I in them." (John 17:25–26)

The Son reveals the Father

"No one knows who the Son is except the Father, or who the Father is except the Son and anyone to whom the Son chooses to reveal him." (Luke 10:22)

APPENDIX B
THE FATHER

John 1:14 And the Word became flesh and dwelt among us, and we have seen his glory, glory as of the only Son from the Father, full of grace and truth.

John 1:18 No one has ever seen God; the only God, who is at the Father's side, he has made him known.

John 3:35 The Father loves the Son and has given all things into his hand.

John 4:21 Jesus said to her, "Woman, believe me, the hour is coming when neither on this mountain nor in Jerusalem will you worship the Father.

John 4:23 The hour is coming, and is now here, when the true worshipers will worship the Father in spirit and truth, for the Father is seeking such people to worship him.

John 5:17 But Jesus answered them, "My Father is working until now, and I am work-ing."

John 5:18 This was why the Jews were seeking all the more to kill him, because not only was he breaking the Sabbath, but he was even calling God his own Father, making himself equal with God.

John 5:19 So Jesus said to them, "Truly, truly, I say to you, the Son can do nothing of his own accord, but only what he sees the Father doing. For whatever the Father does, that the Son does likewise. 20 For the Father loves the Son and shows him all that he himself is doing. And greater works than these will he show him, so that you may marvel. 21 For as the Father raises the dead and gives them life, so also the Son gives life to whom he will. 22 The Father judges no one, but has given all judgment to the Son, 23 that all may honor the Son, just as they honor the Father. Whoever does not honor the Son does not honor the Father who sent him.

John 5:26 As the Father has life in himself, so he has granted the Son also to have life in himself.

John 5:30 "I can do nothing on my own. As I hear, I judge, and my judgment is just, because I seek not my own will but the will of him who sent me. 31 If I alone bear witness about myself, my testimony is not true. 32 There is another who bears wit-ness about me, and I know that the testimony that he bears about me is true.

John 5:36 But the testimony that I have is greater than that of John. For the works that the Father has given me to accomplish, the very works that I am doing, bear witness about me that the Father has sent me. 37 And the Father who sent me has himself borne witness about me. His voice you have never heard, his form you have never seen,

John 5:45 Do not think that I will accuse you to the Father. There is one who accuses you: Moses, on whom you have set your hope.

John 6:27 Do not work for the food that perishes, but for the food that endures to eternal life, which the Son of Man will give to you. For on him God the Father has set his seal."

John 6:32 Jesus then said to them, "Truly, truly, I say to you, it was not Moses who gave you the bread from heaven, but my Father gives you the true bread from heaven.

John 6:37 All that the Father gives me will come to me, and whoever comes to me I will never cast out.

John 6:40 For this is the will of my Father, that everyone who looks on the Son and believes in him should have eternal life, and I will raise him up on the last day."

John 6:42 They said, "Is not this Jesus, the son of Joseph, whose father and mother we know? How does he now say, 'I have come down from heaven'?"

John 6:44 No one can come to me unless the Father who sent me draws him. And I will raise him up on the last day. 45 It is written in the Prophets, 'And they will all be taught by God.' Everyone who has heard and learned from the Father comes to me— 46 not that anyone has seen the Father except he who is from God; he has seen the Father.

John 6:57 As the living Father sent me, and I live because of the Father, so whoever feeds on me, he also will live because of me.

John 6:65 And he said, "This is why I told you that no one can come to me unless it is granted him by the Father."

John 7:14 About the middle of the feast Jesus went up into the temple and began teaching. 15 The Jews therefore marveled, saying, "How is it that this man has learn-ing, when he has never studied?" 16 So Jesus answered them, "My teaching is not mine, but his who sent me. 17 If anyone's will is to do God's will, he will know wheth-er the teaching is from God or whether I am speaking on my own authority. 18 The one who speaks on his own authority seeks his own glory; but the one who seeks the glory of him who sent him is true, and in him there is no falsehood.

John 7:25 Some of the people of Jerusalem therefore said, "Is not this the man whom they seek to kill? 26 And here he is, speaking openly, and they say nothing to him! Can it be that the authorities really know that this is the Christ? 27 But we know where this man comes from, and when the Christ appears, no one will know where he comes from." 28 So Jesus proclaimed, as he taught in the temple, "You know me, and you know where I come from. But I have not come of my own accord. He who sent me is true, and him you do not know. 29 I know him, for I come from him, and he sent me."

John 7:32 The Pharisees heard the crowd muttering these things about him, and the chief priests and Pharisees sent officers to arrest him. 33 Jesus then said, "I will be with you a little longer, and then I am going to him who sent me.

John 8:16 Yet even if I do judge, my judgment is true, for it is not I alone who judge, but I and the Father who sent me.

John 8:18 I am the one who bears witness about myself, and the Father who sent me bears witness about me." 19 They said to him therefore, "Where is your Father?" Jesus answered, "You know neither me nor my Father. If you knew me, you would know my Father also."

John 8:26 I have much to say about you and much to judge, but he who sent me is true, and I declare to the world what I have heard from him." 27 They did not under-stand that he had been speaking to them about the Father.

John 8:28 So Jesus said to them, "When you have lifted up the Son of Man, then you will know that I am he, and that I do nothing on my own authority, but speak just as the Father taught me.

John 8:38 I speak of what I have seen with my Father,

John 8:42 Jesus said to them, "If God were your Father, you would love me, for I came from God and I am here. I came not of my own accord, but he sent me.

John 8:49 Jesus answered, "I do not have a demon, but I honor my Father, and you dishonor me.

John 8:54 Jesus answered, "If I glorify myself, my glory is nothing. It is my Father who glorifies me, of whom you say, 'He is our God.' 55 But you have not known him. I know him. If I were to say that I do not know him, I would be a liar like you, but I do know him and I keep his word.

John 10:15 just as the Father knows me and I know the Father; and I lay down my life for the sheep.

John 10:17 For this reason the Father loves me, because I lay down my life that I may take it up again. 18 No one takes it from me, but I lay it down of my own accord. I have authority to lay it down, and I have authority to take it up again. This charge I have received from my Father."

John 10:29 My Father, who has given them to me, is greater than all, and no one is able to snatch them out of the Father's hand. 30 I and the Father are one."

John 10:32 Jesus answered them, "I have shown you many good works from the Fa-ther; for which of them are you going to stone me?"

John 10:36 do you say of him whom the Father consecrated and sent into the world, 'You are blaspheming,' because I said, 'I am the Son of God'? 37 If I am not doing the works of my Father, then do not believe me; 38 but if I do them, even though you do not believe me, believe the works, that you may know and understand that the Father is in me and I am in the Father."

John 11:41 So they took away the stone. And Jesus lifted up his eyes and said, "Father, I thank you that you have heard me.

John 12:26 If anyone serves me, he must follow me; and where I am, there will my servant be also. If anyone serves me, the Father will honor him. 27 "Now is my soul troubled. And what shall I say? 'Father, save me from this hour'? But for this purpose I have come to this hour. 28 Father, glorify your name." Then a voice came from heaven: "I have glorified it, and I will glorify it again."

John 12:44 And Jesus cried out and said, "Whoever believes in me, believes not in me but in him who sent me. 45 And whoever sees me sees him who sent me.

John 12:49 For I have not spoken on my own authority, but the Father who sent me has himself given me a commandment—what to say and what to speak. 50 And I know that his commandment is eternal life. What I say, therefore, I say as the Father has told me."

John 13:1 Now before the Feast of the Passover, when Jesus knew that his hour had come to depart out of this world to the Father, having loved his own who were in the world, he loved them to the end.

John 13:3 Jesus, knowing that the Father had given all things into his hands, and that he had come from God and was going back to God,

John 13:31 When he had gone out, Jesus said, "Now is the Son of Man glorified, and God is glorified in him. 32 If God is glorified in him, God will also glorify him in him-self, and glorify him at once.

John 14:6 Jesus said to him, "I am the way, and the truth, and the life. No one comes to the Father except through me. 7 If you had known me, you would have known my Father also. From now on you do know him and have seen him." 8 Philip said to him, "Lord, show us the Father, and it is enough for us." 9 Jesus said to him, "Have I been with you so long, and you still do not know me, Philip? Whoever has seen me has seen the Father. How can you say, 'Show us the Father'? 10 Do you not believe that I am in the Father and the Father is in me? The words that I say to you I do not speak on my own authority, but the Father who dwells in me does his works. 11 Believe me that I am in the Father and the Father is in me, or else believe on account of the works themselves. 12 "Truly, truly, I say to you, whoever believes in me will also do the works that I do; and greater works than these will he do, because I am going to the Father. 13 Whatever you ask in my name, this I will do, that the Father may be glorified in the Son.

John 14:16 And I will ask the Father, and he will give you another Helper, to be with you forever,

John 14:20 In that day you will know that I am in my Father, and you in me, and I in you. 21 Whoever has my commandments and keeps them, he it is who loves me. And he who loves me will be loved by my Father, and I will love him and manifest myself to him."

John 14:23 Jesus answered him, "If anyone loves me, he will keep my word, and my Father will love him, and we will come to him and make our home with him.

John 14:26 But the Helper, the Holy Spirit, whom the Father will send in my name, he will teach you all things and bring to your remembrance all that I have said to you.

John 14:28 You heard me say to you, 'I am going away, and I will come to you.' If you loved me, you would have rejoiced, because I am going to the Father, for the Father is greater than I.

John 14:31 but I do as the Father has commanded me, so that the world may know that I love the Father. Rise, let us go from here. 1 "I am the true vine, and my Father is the vinedresser.

John 15:8 By this my Father is glorified, that you bear much fruit and so prove to be my disciples. 9 As the Father has loved me, so have I loved you. Abide in my love.

John 15:15 No longer do I call you servants, for the servant does not know what his master is doing; but I have called you friends, for all that I have heard from my Father I have made known to you. 16 You did not choose me, but I chose you and appointed you that you should go and bear fruit and that your fruit should abide, so that what-ever you ask the Father in my name, he may give it to you.

John 15:23 Whoever hates me hates my Father also. 24 If I had not done among them the works that no one else did, they would not be guilty of sin, but now they have seen and hated both me and my Father.

John 15:26 "But when the Helper comes, whom I will send to you from the Father, the Spirit of truth, who proceeds from the Father, he will bear witness about me.

John 16:3 And they will do these things because they have not known the Father, nor me.

John 16:10 concerning righteousness, because I go to the Father, and you will see me no longer;

John 16:15 All that the Father has is mine; therefore I said that he will take what is mine and declare it to you.

John 16:17 So some of his disciples said to one another, "What is this that he says to us, 'A little while, and you will not see me, and again a little while, and you will see me'; and, 'because I am going to the Father'?"

John 16:23 In that day you will ask nothing of me. Truly, truly, I say to you, whatever you ask of the Father in my name, he will give it to you.

John 16:25 "I have said these things to you in figures of speech. The hour is coming when I will no longer speak to you in figures of speech but will tell you plainly about the Father. 26 In that day you will ask in my name, and I do not say to you that I will ask the Father on your behalf; 27 for the Father himself loves you, because you have loved me and have believed that I came from God. 28 I came from the Father and have come into the world, and now I am leaving the world and going to the Father."

John 16:32 Behold, the hour is coming, indeed it has come, when you will be scattered, each to his own home, and will leave me alone. Yet I am not alone, for the Father is with me.

John 17:1 When Jesus had spoken these words, he lifted up his eyes to heaven, and said, "Father, the hour has come; glorify your Son that the Son may glorify you,

John 17:5 And now, Father, glorify me in your own presence with the glory that I had with you before the world existed.

John 17:11 And I am no longer in the world, but they are in the world, and I am com-ing to you. Holy Father, keep them in your name, which you have given me, that they may be one, even as we are one.

John 17:21 that they may all be one, just as you, Father, are in me, and I in you, that they also may be in us, so that the world may believe that you have sent me.

John 17:24 Father, I desire that they also, whom you have given me, may be with me where I am, to see my glory that you have given me because you loved me before the foundation of the world. 25 O righteous Father, even though the world does not know you, I know you, and these know that you have sent me.

John 18:11 So Jesus said to Peter, "Put your sword into its sheath; shall I not drink the cup that the Father has given me?"

John 20:17 Jesus said to her, "Do not cling to me, for I have not yet ascended to the Father; but go to my brothers and say to them, 'I am ascending to my Father and your Father, to my God and your God.'"

John 20:21 Jesus said to them again, "Peace be with you. As the Father has sent me, even so I am sending you."

More Building Faith Family Resources

ABOUT THE AUTHOR

Steve Demme and his wife Sandra have been married since 1979. They have been blessed with four sons, three lovely daughters-in-law, and three special grandchildren.

Steve has served in full or part time pastoral ministry for many years after graduating from Gordon-Conwell Theological Seminary. He is the creator of Math-U-See and the founder of Building Faith Families and has served on the board of Joni and Friends, PA.

He produces a monthly newsletter, weekly podcasts, and regular posts https://www.facebook.com/stevedemme/

Steve is a regular speaker at home education conferences, men's ministry events, and family retreats. His desire is to strengthen, teach, encourage, validate, and exhort parents and families to follow the biblical model for the Christian home.

BUILDING FAITH FAMILIES

Exists to teach and encourage families to embrace the biblical model for the Christian home.

Scripture declares God created the sacred institution of the family. In His wisdom, He designed marriage to be between one man and one woman. We believe healthy God-fearing families are the basic building block for the church and society.

The family is foundational and transformational. Parents and children become more like Jesus as they lay their lives down for each other, pray for each other, and learn to love each other as God has loved them.

RESOURCES TO ENCOURAGE AND STRENGTHEN YOUR FAMILY

- The **Monthly Newsletter** is an encouraging exhortation as well as updates on Bible contests and upcoming speaking engagements.

- **Podcast** Each week an episode is released on our website, Itunes, and our Facebook page. These may be downloaded for free.

- **Seminars for free download** For over 20 years Steve has been speaking and teaching at conferences around the world. Many of his messages are available for your edification.

- **Like us on Facebook** for updates of new podcasts, speaking engagements, and new resources for your home and family.

www.buildingfaithfamilies.org

CRISIS TO CHRIST,

THE HARDEST AND BEST YEAR OF MY LIFE

I have wounds, scars, baggage, and stuff from my past, which I have tried to ignore, but which is always present. In 2012 I was confronted with the distressing knowledge that my own wounds, which I thought were hidden and of no consequence, were wounding those closest to me, my wife and sons.

I discovered I cannot hide my toxic issues for eventually they will leak out and hurt those who are closest to me, primarily my wife and children.

This difficult time, the hardest and best year of my life, was instrumental in changing my life and transforming my relationship with God and my family. On this journey I experienced pain which led me to acknowledge my own hurts and get help from the body of Christ to understand root causes of my distress and confront unbiblical thinking.

While I experienced incredible pain, I also discovered that my Heavenly Dad likes me just the way I am. Even though my path went through deep waters, God was with me every step of the way.

My motivation in writing is to affirm others who are going through similar valleys and tribulations. These hard journeys are normal for the Christian. Every person of note in scripture endured at least one life changing crisis. God uses these difficult times to work deep in our hearts, reveal more of Himself, and transform us into the image of His Son.

TRANSFORMED IN LOVE,

LOVING OTHERS AS JESUS HAS LOVED US

John 15:9 revealed God not only loved the world, He loved me. Jesus says to His disciples, "As the Father has loved me, so have I loved you. Abide in my love." Just as the Father loved His Son, Jesus loves me the same way.

The secret to abiding in God's love is found in the next few verses. "If you keep my commandments, you will abide in my love, just as I have kept my Father's commandments and abide in His love. This is my commandment, that you love one another as I have loved you." (John 15:10, 12)

As I love others, as I have been loved, I will abide in the love of God. As a husband and father, my primary responsibilities are to love God, my wife, and my sons. I am writing as a man and sharing how God has led me to begin applying these principles in our home. But these principles are applicable to every believer.

The fruit of loving others as we have been loved will not only bless each of our homes, but our communities as well. "By this all people will know that you are my disciples, if you have love for one another." (John 13:34)

As family members pray for one another, bear each other's burdens, lay their lives down for each other, and learn to love one another as Jesus has loved them, they are transformed and become more like Jesus.

SPEAKING THE TRUTH IN LOVE,

LESSONS I'VE LEARNED ABOUT
FAMILY COMMUNICATION

Most of what I've learned about communication, I acquired in the past few years during transitioning my business to a family owned business. The ability to communicate about difficult topics like business, values, your occupation, and a family's legacy takes effort and training.

As a husband and father, I have the potential to build up and encourage my family like no one else. I also have the ability to tear down and discourage my wife and sons. The Bible teaches effective principles of communication which are timeless.

My relationship with my wife and children has been transformed through godly safe communication. As I continue to grow in grace and the knowledge of God, I am in a better place to have open, transparent, and honest communication. While the skills we have acquired in being a clear speaker and an engaged listener are beneficial, investing time to have a quiet heart is essential. For out of the abundance of the heart, the mouth speaks.

I hope the principles we have learned and applied to such benefit in our own home and business will be a help to you on your journey. May the words of our mouth and the meditation of our heart be acceptable in your sight, O LORD, our Rock and our Redeemer. (from Psalms 19:14)

THE CHRISTIAN HOME
AND FAMILY WORSHIP

In this readable and encouraging book, Steve shares practical scripture-based tips for teaching the word of God to children of all ages.

He also addresses common obstacles we all face in establishing the discipline of regular family worship.

Be encouraged by Steve's experiences teaching his four sons, and learn from other families who share strategies that have worked for their children. You may purchase this book, or participate in our Family Worship Challenge.

When you read or listen to *"The Christian Home and Family Worship"* within 30 days of receiving your copy, it is yours for FREE. If you are unable to fulfill this obligation, you agree to send a check for $50.00 to Building Faith Families. Steve will follow up with you at the end of thirty days. Contact Steve at sdemme@demmelearning.com

"I loved the book and read it in about a week and a half. My chief take-away was family worship needs to be an important part of family life. I've had five family worship times and I can definitely say I've already seen some fruits from these sessions. Your book had some great examples of how to make it more appealing to the kids."

"I was indeed able to read the book in time. The main thing I took away from it was the Nike slogan: "Just do it." So I did.

STEWARDSHIP

"Where your treasure is, there will your heart be also." (Luke 12:34)

There are two components addressed in Stewardship, our treasure and our heart. God calls us to love Him with all our heart and be faithful stewards of our God-given treasure. Half of the curriculum is focused on our relationship with God and the other half with being wise stewards of our treasure. It is appropriate for anyone with a good grasp of basic math and who has completed Algebra 1.

Stewardship Instruction Pack
The Stewardship Instruction Pack contains the instruction manual with lesson-by-lesson instructions, detailed solutions, and the DVD with lesson-by-lesson video instruction.

Discipleship Material
Steve references hundreds of scriptures from Genesis to Revelation in sharing how God has helped him to apply biblical principles in his home, business, and personal walk with God. He also shares a plethora of topical studies on essential components of discipleship. Students are encouraged to read the complete New Testament during the course as well.

STEWARDSHIP

Stewardship Student Pack

The Stewardship Student Pack contains the Student Workbook with lesson-by-lesson worksheets, and review pages. It also includes the Stewardship Tests.

A Sampling of "Treasure Topics"

- Earning Money
- Taxes
- Banking and Interest
- Credit Cards
- Comparison Shopping
- Costs for Operating an Automobile
- Wise Charitable Giving
- Starting Your Own Business, and more

A Taste of "Heart Studies"

- The Love of Money
- Trusting God and Being Content
- Purchase with Prayer
- Work is a God Thing
- Our Identity in Christ
- The Inspired Word of God
- Honor Your Father and Mother
- Guard Your Heart

Thanks for this curriculum! This was the best math course I've taken in all my high school years, and I don't even like math :)

- Caleb

That your curriculum is Christ-centered has made the biggest difference in my homeschool experience.

- Sarah

THE HYMNS FOR FAMILY WORSHIP

This time-honored collection of 100 classic hymns will be a rich addition to your family worship. Make a joyful noise to the LORD!

In addition to the music for these carefully selected songs of worship, the history and origin of each hymn enhances the meaning of the lyrics.

There are four CDs with piano accompaniment for singing along in your home, car, or church.

Some of the titles are:

- What a Friend We Have in Jesus
- Holy, Holy, Holy
- It Is Well With My Soul
- To God Be The Glory
- All Hail the Power of Jesus Name
- Amazing Grace
- How Firm a Foundation
- Blessed Assurance
- Christ Arose
- Rise Up O Men of God
- Jesus Paid It All
- Just As I Am, along with 88 more!